Big Travel
Small Budget

How to Travel More,
Spend Less, and See the World

RYAN SHAUERS

Disclaimer and FTC Notice

ISBN: 0692531866
ISBN-13: 978-0692531860

DEDICATION

To all of you who not only read this book
but actually put it into action …

RESOURCES AND LINKS

Thanks for purchasing the paperback edition of Big Travel, Small Budget. I hope this book becomes dog-earred, highlighted, and beat up as you take it across time zones and international borders. Inside, you'll see a number of references to books, blog posts, websites and other resources. But here's the funny thing: you can't easily click on links in a print book, so rather than list each URL in the text, I've compiled them all, organized by chapter, on my site. You can visit the Big Travel resource page at:

www.desktodirtbag.com/bigtravel-paperback

CONTENTS

FOREWARD

A few years back I was on the edge. I was in a job I hated, and I had this insatiable wanderlust that I knew would only be quelled by hopping on a plane and going somewhere exotic.

But I couldn't do that, right?

I wore a suit and tie to work everyday. I had bills and responsibilities. "Travel is only for business-people and retirees," I remember telling myself. And more importantly, travel was expensive—and I wasn't exactly rolling in Benjamins at the time.

For a year, my desktop background was a photo of a beach bungalow in Koh Samui, Thailand that was overlooking the ocean. This served as a constant reminder of what I wanted but at the same time was something that seemed so unbelievably far away.

However, if you visualize something for long enough, the world has a funny way of conspiring in your favor.
After spending months working up the courage and putting my financial concerns aside, I finally left my job and moved to Thailand for 7 months.

It was the time of my life, and it set the stage for a life of entrepreneurship and travel that I simply didn't know was possible during my time as a desk jockey.

The biggest surprise? Travel didn't have to be expensive.

In fact my Thailand adventure (and other subsequent adventures in Bali, Boracay, and various other exotic places), ended up being cheaper than if I'd stayed home.
But there's a right and a wrong way to do this. I did it on my own and largely learned from trial and error.

You don't have to.

I've been following Ryan's travels for the last 3 years, and the amount of hands on experience and knowledge he has about traveling on a budget, hacking deals, and proving that the American Dream is more than a white picket fence is second to none.

In these pages you'll find a roadmap to adventure. You'll find ways to cross off bucket list items. You'll find ways to live in the lap of luxury for next to nothing. You'll learn about how the power of community has completely shifted the art of both long-term and short-term travel.

These unconventional strategies for traveling on the cheap represent a marked shift in society, where combining technology and a willingness to try something different, leads to something most could only dream about even a decade to go.

Don't just read this book. Apply the things you learn in it, and go have the adventure of a lifetime. That's what I'm doing, and I know that's what Ryan would want you to do as well.

Remember, there are only seven days in a week, and "someday" isn't one of them.

— Sean Ogle

Location180.com | LocationRebel.com

PREFACE

First and foremost I have to thank Andrea for putting up with me as I became totally enveloped in this daunting project of writing a book. Maybe it gets easier with subsequent efforts, but just the thought of "writing a book" can be overwhelming. I spent the better part of most days engrossed in this project (or procrastinating), as we house sat in the remote mountains of Baja California, Mexico—which was the perfect place to get some real work done.

Thanks, of course, to my family for putting up with all my adventures over the years, and sorry Mom for putting you through those sleepless nights from my time in the Middle East, in Medellin, or in Mexico.

Of course, a huge thanks to all my readers of my blog over the past few years. Who would have ever imagined that I'd still be going this long? In part, it truly is because of all of you.

I first really even contemplated the idea of writing a book as I watched the successes of Lise Cartwright and Carlo Cretaro, both fellow members of Location Rebel, in launching their Kindle books and for sharing in great detail how they did it and how everything turned out for them. Being around other people doing remarkable things encourages you to do remarkable things.

Big thanks to Terry O'Connor and Anita Agarwal in my (now defunct) weekly mastermind group who initially encouraged me to go forward with a book while I was living in Medellin. I let the ball drop on that one (though I still have the manuscript). The encouragement got me moving in the right direction and eventually led me to putting this book out. Being around a supportive crowd is one of the most important things you can find because you won't even attempt what you don't think is possible.

Millions of thanks to a few of my friends and followers who suffered through the earliest draft of this book and helped me identify the weaknesses, improve my voice, and expand on crucial missing elements. Thank you Dave Sandel, Colin Price, Rob Henkel, Adam Marcus, Anna Filipski, Ryan Cunico, Jen Chien, Katie Bowles, Jean, Jason Matthews, Faith Meckley, Adam Nutting, Amber Hardesty, and Sofia Pastoriza. You all helped me get this book to a place where I felt comfortable and confident passing it off to an editor.

CHAPTER 1

INTRODUCTION TO YOUR PRACTICAL AND TACTICAL ROADMAP

Is This a Dream?

We bobbed in the warm tropical waters along the beach in Loreto, Mexico. The sun had just set, but the faint bands of clouds were still lit up in ribbons of orange, red, and yellow. Children squealed with delight as they splashed in the water nearby with their parents, vendors strolled along the malecon *[boardwalk] selling cold drinks, and the full moon illuminated the still water while kayakers passed by.*

I was there with my girlfriend, Andrea, whom I had met the year before while living in Colombia, but I found myself lost in my thoughts as I looked out over the water. We had just wrapped up an incredible day on a private tour around Coronado Island off the coast, watching small pods of dolphins swim by, snorkeling in the crystal

1

clear waters with hundreds of colorful fish, and gawking at blue-footed boobies and seals with our guide, Genaro.

Since leaving Colombia we had traveled from the beaches and theme parks of Florida to the frozen north of Fairbanks, Alaska for the Northern Lights and dog sledding. Over just the past few months, we had driven together from rainy Seattle across the American West to more than 17 National Parks and continued south to the sun-soaked beaches of Mexico.

"Que estas pensando?" [What are you thinking?] Andrea asked me, knocking me out of my trance.

"Just what an amazing day we had and what a crazy adventure this has been . . . It's all kinda hard to believe," I responded in Spanish.

"Ah si. Absolutamente increible!"

I then realized that all of those adventures had only just happened in the past eight months . . . which is to say nothing of the incredible past two and a half years it has been since I initially walked away from the nine-to-five, so I could travel more.

I had to pinch myself floating there in the crystal blue water to make sure I wasn't dreaming.

Breaking Away . . . But Not Breaking the Bank

In the frenetic pace of today's world, it's difficult for most people to break away for a week-long vacation. When they do manage to get away, they end up breaking the bank during their travels, which in turn leads them to believe that long-term travel is a luxury held exclusively for the rich. The truth of the matter is that traveling for a few weeks or even a few months doesn't have to be expensive. I've traveled for a month for much less than my cost of living while working a steady job, and for much less than I used to spend on week-long vacations.

In this book I'm going to show you exactly how I have managed to save thousands of dollars on transportation and accommodation during the past few years of continuous travel. Being on the road since January 2013 has been one of the greatest experiences of my life and has taken me in so many new and unexpected directions, including the launch of my blog, writing this book, and so many other adventures. It's been truly remarkable sharing my journey and connecting with so many like-minded people.

I regularly hear from readers who wish they could follow in my footsteps and embark on their own long-term adventures, but their biggest roadblock almost always comes down to money. I wrote this book as a practical and tactical roadmap to dramatically reducing your expenses and making long-term travel more affordable for everyone, regardless of your starting budget. All it takes is a little know-how mixed with creativity, and a world of travel will open up to you as the reward.

When I worked a nine-to-five job, I was allowed to take only a single week of vacation at a time, and thus, I would try to jam in as much as possible. I'd come back from vacation somewhat wiped out and with a considerable hole in my savings account. It was only after leaving my job at the end of 2012 and embarking on a year-long sabbatical that I began to embrace the methods I'll be describing in this book and to truly realize that long-term travel is much more affordable than my previous everyday life—so affordable, in fact, that I continued traveling beyond my initially planned year and have experimented with many different ways to save money while living a life of travel and adventure.

The Best of the Best

Some tactics worked well, others not so much. What follows are the best of the best—the big wins that will get you out there traveling in a way you never imagined. Now, you don't necessarily need to become a permanent vagabond like I did in order to reap the benefits of affordable travel that I will be sharing in the following pages, but you certainly can if you like. Most of these principles can be applied toward a two-week vacation from your regular job or can be scaled up to fit the time you have to spare, which is something that becomes especially appealing if you are going to be between jobs or would like to make the transition to freelancing.

I promise that if you implement just one of the tactics that I share in the following chapters, you will be able to save at least a few hundred dollars during your travels. But more important than just saving money is the realization that you can finally make your travel dreams come true, even on a limited budget. Stepping away from the daily grind of work will allow you to take your life back, open yourself up to new experiences and perspectives, and fundamentally change your idea of what is possible, what is important, and where your priorities stand.

Don't be the person who puts off their dreams to break free until retirement. Be the kind of person that makes your friends and family stop and say, "I don't know how they do it." Be the kind of person that doesn't just talk about how they like to travel, but truly makes it a priority in life.

Money definitely isn't everything in life, but money is almost always the biggest perceived obstacle to travel. Let's mitigate some of those worries and make travel a reality by doing it smarter, cheaper, and longer.

The methods we're about to get into have been proven to help people realize their goals of travel and adventure, which they previously thought were financially beyond their means. You'll read anecdotes about some other savvy travelers whom I've met in my travels or who have connected with me via my blog. Each chapter will provide you with a different actionable approach where you can save money and stretch your budget during your trip.

Forget the Top Ramen
Each tactic, simply used alone, will amount to significant savings—we are not going to be talking about saving a dollar here or there by eating Top Ramen in the hostel dorm room. But better still, some of these tactics can be combined to create a synergistic effect where you can take

mind-bogglingly awesome trips for a fraction of what you would otherwise pay. Your friends and family will be blown away, jealous, and asking you, "How can you afford all that?"

Are you ready?

Not to Brag, But . . .

Everyone always asks me how I've been able to stay on the road for so long . . . Since walking away from my desk job in December 2012, I spent nearly a year road-tripping more than 20,000 miles across the American West, seeing some of the most awe-inspiring places I've ever laid eyes on. I set out backpacking across Colombia before settling down in the vibrant city of Medellin. Most recently, I've headed out for another major road trip across international borders.

Indeed, somehow, some way, I've been able to maintain a life of adventure and travel over the past few years, and I have no immediate plans to return to the traditional world of work.

I don't say that to brag, but just to show you that you too can create more opportunities to travel in your life and can stretch your budget over the long term, or at least much longer than you probably anticipate.

When I was working the nine-to-five as a legislative assistant in Washington, DC (actually, it was nine-to-six, with plenty of much, much later nights), I would constantly be waiting for the weekend, so grateful when a three-day weekend came about that would allow me to drive a little farther out, and the Holy Grail, a week-long vacation to the mountains and Mother Nature once or twice a year.

I love the outdoors, travel, and adventure, along with the constant unknown and uncertainty of where the day's adventures might take you when you are traveling. It doesn't really matter whether you are traveling domestically or internationally, it's all about stepping away from the daily grind that opens you up to new perspectives and places.

Fruition of the "Someday" Plan

I would save a little money every month, putting it away for "someday," but there were never any concrete plans laid, and I always thought I needed to save "just a little more" before making the jump.

I was finally forced into making a decision when my boss announced he was going to retire at the end of the year (effectively ending my job) . . . I would either make the leap into what I'd been longing for, all those days daydreaming at my desk, or, like everybody else, I would start the frantic search for a similar job and keep putting my dreams off until an uncertain date in the future.

I was lucky in many ways because I was forced to take action. I know from my own experience that it is much easier to forever delay taking action . . . You can always save up just a little more, and there's almost never, ever a perfect time to uproot your life to travel. That's why almost every story like this begins with someone getting fired, downsized, or losing their job—it's so much easier to remain forever complacent (not bad, but not great), than to take the risk of walking away to travel, or heading out on your own and forging your own path.

Stepping away from the nine-to-five was one of the best things I've ever done. It's allowed me to take a mental breather, leave behind the stress of work, and live simply while pursuing the things that interest me and not just pursuing money. I felt like I got my life back, and it gave me a new perspective on what is important to me and what is possible when you commit to taking a leap. In the process I've discovered skills and passions that I never knew I had, as well as rekindling passions that I had let die out because I used to be too busy. By taking this path, you'll come across side trails that branch out to places you never imagined or knew existed when you set out from the trailhead.

The Leap

If you're looking at making the leap into the world of long-term travel, I'm here to tell you that it is totally possible—but, more importantly, it is totally worth it. One of the top five regrets of the dying is "I wish I hadn't worked so hard." Who regrets the opportunity to travel more?

There are tons of people that inspired and informed me in the years before I made the jump, and I'm hoping to do the same for you.

Maybe you hope to travel for just six months but don't think you have enough cash on hand. The info in this book will teach you how to make a smaller budget last over a longer period.

Maybe you hope to stretch your six-month budget into a full year. The same principles hold true.

Whether you hope to travel more domestically and see the things you've always wanted to or you would like to dive into a foreign culture feet first, there is something here for you.

The tactics in this book also apply equally to retirees or recent college graduates.

If anything, I've been crafty with my travels this whole time, which has allowed me to keep traveling. That's what I want to share with you.

Long-term travel is not the exclusive domain of the rich, and there are countless stories unfolding from fellow vagabonds all over the world that prove that simply isn't true.

I planned to set out for a yearlong adventure at the beginning of 2013, a year of climbing, backpacking, and hiking across the American West—doing the things I loved to do every weekend, but doing them on a daily basis with a constantly changing horizon. I'd enjoy my career sabbatical and then head back to the "real world."

Multiple people warned me when I set out down this path that my travels would fundamentally change me and I wouldn't want to return to the regular desk job.

Well, they were right, I'm still out here. Now I should probably give you the same warning.

Who Wants to Travel?

You ask 10 people what they like to do, and nine of them will probably mention traveling. Most everybody loves to travel, see new things, and get away from the daily grind. Some people like the big cities, some like beaches, and some like remote country escapes.

If you've picked up this book, I'm going to assume it's because you are seriously interested in traveling more but don't quite know how to make it happen besides having "more money." And we're not just talking about a week or two here and there but breaking away for a longer stretch of time.

The Simple Vacation v. Long-Term Travel

First of all, let's differentiate long-term travel as being something quite different from a simple vacation. A vacation is just that, a short trip, a break from your day-to-day life while long-term travel allows you to step far away from the tedious monotony of work, offering you a means to really recognize with clarity what is important and unimportant to you.

It allows you to experience so many new things and learn more about yourself, your perseverance, your tolerance to risk and unfamiliar environments, and much more in a whole new way.

Of course, travel is not the only way to realize those benefits (though it is one of the best ways). Nor is travel a panacea that will fix all your problems. And despite your romantic notions while daydreaming at your desk, the journey won't always be perfect either.

I'm remembering that time my buddy Jeff got bit by a cat on a remote Colombian beach and we began to worry about the possibility of rabies with all the bats flying overhead. Then there was that time I got terribly sick passing through Death Valley and had to hole up at my camp site in the sweltering heat all afternoon in misery.

What I wouldn't have given for a couch, air conditioning, and a Netflix account at that moment! And many, many other misadventures.

Yes, there will be bad days, ups and downs, problems to overcome, and crises to handle while you travel. But those things are going to happen along the traditional path as well. What you bring back from long-term travel will shape you for years to come and is well worth a few difficult patches.

No matter what sort of trip you are embarking on, it is very different being on the road for half a year versus stepping away for just a week or two. Long-term travel permits you to take off the rose-colored glasses of a tourist and really immerse yourself in the lifestyle and place, for both the good and the bad. It is, for lack of a better analogy, the difference between going somewhere for spring break or studying abroad there.

I would define long-term travel as being something at least six months in length. Whether you are traveling domestically or internationally, anything under three months just sort of feels like a long vacation. You don't really get into the groove and reap the biggest benefits of long-term travel until you get to that 4–6 month range, in my experience.

Long-term travel is not an escape from the "real world." It is experiencing the real world on your own terms without the confines (and comfort) of your present job, social circle, physical possessions, self-limiting beliefs, etc.

Long-term travel is so much more than a vacation, and while I realize that long-term travel isn't something that everyone prioritizes, it is something that I think everyone should do at least once in life. The so-called "gap year" can be a tremendously fulfilling experience, which sadly isn't that common in the United States.

26 Years of Vacation

The average American worker receives about 2–3 weeks of

paid vacation time per year (if they're lucky). Because our time for vacations is so limited, we feel compelled to go on whirlwind trips, trying to cram everything we can into those trips. Five countries in Europe in a week? Done! Fly into Costa Rica and pack in a week of adventure sports? Done! Road trip a few thousand miles and cram in five National Parks? Done!

When you want to hurry something, that means you no longer care about it and want to get on to other things.

—Robert M. Pirsig in *Zen and the Art of Motorcycle Maintenance*

Take a few selfies to prove you were there, now you can check the box that you've "done" Europe or Yosemite or Machu Picchu.

These vacations tend to not only be expensive but also a little exhausting. This is not the type of travel I will be talking about in this book, but rather a much more affordable and less frenetic pace of travel that is sustainable for months on end.

Indeed, most people will spend more in a single week-long vacation than what we'll be looking to spend over the course of a month.

Vacations are expensive, but long-term travel definitely need not be.

Just taking a career break or sabbatical for six months would allow you to travel the equivalent of the average American's 13 years of vacation time (at two weeks per year), and a one-year sabbatical would be equal to 26 years worth of travel and vacation.

I think this point really deserves repeating: *You could take the equivalent of 26 years worth of vacation time in one amazing gap year.*

That is equal to your annual vacations between the ages of 30 and 56, essentially the bulk of your adult working years.

Let that sink in for a moment . . .

Imagine . . .

Imagine all you could see, learn, accomplish and experience in that time if you were able to refocus those 8+ hours per day of work on something else, something of more personal significance to you. You could become a better cook, learn to play guitar, learn a new language, or write a book.

Most people immediately dismiss the notion that they could afford to get away for that long. "That must be nice, but I could never do that."

No matter whether you are rich or poor, time is the most precious commodity that each of us possesses—whether that means more time with family, time traveling, or time pursuing your hobbies and what you are truly passionate about.

We are going to kick your money excuses to the curb and open doors that you didn't know were there, so then the real questions become:

Can you afford to keep putting off your dreams to travel?
Can you really afford not to take this time off?

Big Chapter, Small Summary

- "Long-term travel" means traveling for at least 6 months; allowing you to really immerse yourself in a place, culture, and the travel lifestyle.
- Traveling in this way offers an inexpensive path to a rich life. You don't have to actually be rich.
- Spend your most precious resource (time) developing yourself and doing more of what you actually want to do.
- Make your someday be today.

CHAPTER 2

MONEY—IT'S A DRAG

The Trust Fund Kid . . . Yeah Right!

I was camped out on the shores of Lake Mead outside of Las Vegas, Nevada, having arrived late the night before. I awoke to a sun-parched landscape along the banks of an ever-receding reservoir. A thick, white line wrapped around the shore like rings on a bathtub.

As I was finishing up my breakfast, I was approached by two older guys who were both camped out nearby.

Lake Mead, it turns out, is fairly popular with the older retiree crowd that likes to gather there and drink away their social security checks. One of the old guys was friendly enough, and we eventually got to talking about how I was taking a year off to travel around the country.

Chuckling, he snidely retorted to his friend, "Oh yeah, his daddy's got money, that's how he's out here."

Ha! If only.

The Money Crowd

Everybody thinks that you've got to come from a family

with money and have a trust fund to be able to set out for anything longer than the normal couple weeks of vacation per year. But I'm here to tell you that nothing could be further from the truth. You don't have to do things the "normal" way.

I've met dozens and dozens of long-term vagabonds during my travels and not a single one of them comes from a family of money (at least not that I know). Most are simply thrifty, resourceful, and find ways to make it work by living within a budget, taking pleasure in the simple things, and above all by prizing their personal freedom over material things.

To find yourself traveling with the money crowd, you would probably need to be summering in the Hamptons, clubbing in Ibiza, or sailing your yacht off of Monaco. That is definitely not my style of travel or what this book is about.

You don't need to have a trust fund, and you don't need to be a millionaire in order to travel.

The Millionaire Fantasy

Besides, nobody actually wants to have one million dollar bills sitting in a bank somewhere, as Tim Ferriss observed in *The 4-Hour Work Week*: "People don't want to be millionaires—they want to experience what they believe only millions can buy. . . . $1,000,000 in the bank isn't the fantasy. The fantasy is the lifestyle of complete freedom it supposedly allows."

You can live on a beach in some tropical paradise with a cleaning lady, a cook, and all those things for surprisingly little money if that's what you really want.

When you boil down the millionaire fantasy, it usually comes down to working less and having more freedom, which also equals less worries and stress. They want the freedom to travel and to do what they want, when they want. That's exactly what we're after here.

You don't have to wait until you win the lottery or hit it
rich to finally travel.

The alternative is to write your own winning lottery ticket,
not by the sudden accumulation of wealth but the gradual
reduction to what you decide is essential for your life.

—Chris Guillebeau in *The Art of Non-Conformity*

I began my yearlong sabbatical with money that I had
saved over the course of working the traditional nine-to-
five job, which is the model that probably 95% of travelers
follow. Work, save money, travel until they run out of
cash, and then go back to work. There's absolutely nothing
wrong with that approach. Indeed, it is the most
conventional and probably the most palatable way to go
about doing it.

I have met people who have embarked on overseas
travel with just a few hundred dollars to their names and
they used that need, that burning necessity to make
enough money to eat and live, to launch themselves full
bore into entrepreneurial activities in their newfound
homes overseas. Nothing like sink or swim! Maybe that
approach will work best for you.

The Million-Dollar Question

But for the rest of us, here's the million-dollar question:
*How much money do you really need to have saved up in order to
embark on a thrifty but fulfilling long-term trip?*

It's the question that everybody wants to know but is
also one of the hardest to answer, without knowing what
style of traveler you are and not knowing what type of trip
you are interested in.

–Will you be traveling overseas to the more expensive

capital cities of Europe?

–Will you be traveling to the more budget friendly locales of Southeast Asia or Latin America?

–Will you be constantly on the go, or do you prefer to hunker down in a place to get to know it?

–Will you be camping across the American West? Or will you be out clubbing in Las Vegas?

–Are you traveling solo, as a couple, or with a family?

You are going to have to do your due diligence and find out further details from people who have embarked on similar travels while basing it on what you know about yourself as a traveler and your personal preferences.

Many bloggers publish detailed expense reports (myself included) for their travels and adventures, so just find someone out there doing what you want to do, whether it is sailing across the Pacific, backpacking Europe, or driving their motorcycle across the Americas, and start asking questions.

Some General Guidelines

I'm going to set some general guidelines here based upon my style of traveling, which will provide a good launching point for you.

I don't exclusively seek out the cheapest of everything. I travel first and foremost to enjoy things, see new places, try new food, experience new things, and learn more about the world. I eat out on a semi-regular basis. I don't find the absolute cheapest possible place to sleep if I'll be staying in a hotel or hostel, but I also don't spend top dollar on lodging. I'm not a luxury traveler by any means. I like simple but comfortable when it comes to my travels, and I indulge in splurges from time to time.

I enjoy traveling off the beaten path (my third time flying overseas was to live in Yemen for half a year), and I prize deeply immersing myself in a place rather than superficially passing through (slower travel, which is also more conducive to affordable travel). I like to keep things open-ended and flexible for those serendipitous moments.

I try to measure my expenditures while traveling by basing it on what I could do with that money instead. If a hotel costs $100 per night in San Diego, I ask myself what else I could use that money for down the road by staying some place cheaper. There have been other times where I've spent $200 for a (once in a lifetime) chance to dine at the upscale molecular gastronomy restaurant, El Cielo, which included a bottle of wine and 20 "moments" (courses of a meal, but there were some that were exclusively sensory and not to eat).

Sometimes the expense is worth it, other times you may decide that it isn't.

I have the money to travel because I have prioritized my spending to enable travel—not on a shiny new car, upscale apartment, or a big TV with 250+ channels. My girlfriend, Andrea, is from Colombia where they make far, far less than Western countries (the average monthly income is only $692), yet she has been able to take a year off to travel with me across the United States and Central America because she made it a priority, saved money, and committed to making it happen.

The key, no matter your income or goals, is to embrace conscious spending at all times . . . both while saving to travel and while you are traveling.

Spend extravagantly on the things you love, and cut costs mercilessly on the things you don't. This book isn't about telling you to stop buying lattes. Instead, it's about being able to actually spend more on the things you love by not spending money on all the knucklehead things you don't care about.

—Ramit Sethi in *I Will Teach You to be Rich*

My Rule of Thumb

From my conversations with other long-term travelers and from my various methods of traveling from road-tripping across the American West, to backpacking and living in South America, I've found that a good general rule of thumb is about $1,200 per month, which provides a good baseline for most budget travelers. This amount is based solely around travel and does not take into account other outside expenditures ranging from insurance, student loan payments, and so forth.

Many months I end up spending less than $1,000 in expenditures thanks to some of the tactics in this book. But there were other times where I would go over that amount either due to unexpected costs or embarking on periods of more intensive traveling. Over the long term, I still base my planning around $1,200 per month.

Even if you do spend less overall (which is the goal here), it is nice to have a built-in buffer of a few hundred dollars for planning purposes. It's much better to surprise yourself about how far the money is going and be able to travel for a little longer, than it is to find your trip cut drastically short because you didn't account for unexpected expenses or you were going out much more than you anticipated. Twelve-hundred dollars per month, or $40 per day, also coincidentally happens to align quite well with the US federal minimum wage earnings if you were to work 40 hours a week. Yes, you can live a life of full-time travel on the equivalent of minimum wage.

I've met many people who are able to travel on half that per day, such as those who temporarily call Southeast Asia home and are able to live on $600 per month with a fairly high standard of living. We will aim to replicate their low cost of living but in other parts of the world that aren't quite as affordable.

For planning purposes, let's shoot for $1,200 per month for at least six months, or $7,200. With that sort of money, you can easily plan to break away for at least a six-month adventure and stretch it even longer by utilizing some of the tactics I give you in this book.

I will be breaking down the $1,200 per month figure as it relates to each tactic in the chapters ahead, which will also help you judge your projected costs in relation to mine.

These numbers are meant to provide you with a framework, but please don't get caught up on the specific amount you have on hand or the exact cost per month (which you're probably going to do anyway). In this book we are going to focus on getting the maximum returns possible for your limited budget, no matter what your starting point is.

Ultimately, you may well discover that vagabonding on the cheap becomes your favorite way to travel, even if given more expensive options. Indeed, not only does simplicity save you money and buy you time; it also makes you more adventuresome, forces you into sincere contact with locals, and allows you the independence to follow your passions and curiosities down exciting new roads.

— Rolf Potts in *Vagabonding*

Now that we've defined what sort of travel book this is and what sort of travel experience we'll be targeting, let's dive into the specific ways we can have Big Travel on a Small Budget.

Time to hit the road . . .

Big Chapter, Small Summary
- Very few long-term travelers are millionaires or even particularly wealthy.

- A good rule of thumb is to expect to budget about $1,200 per month, but don't get caught up by a number. The goal is to stretch our budget no matter the starting point.
- The type of traveler you are and style of travel you are interested in will determine how much money you'll need.
- The most important point is to embrace conscious spending in all aspects of your life.

CHAPTER 3

GO BY LAND

Intruders in the Night

Andrea prodded me awake in the middle of the night. "Listen! Do you hear that?!" she asked me worriedly. We were camped in my truck in the Alabama Hills below the towering Sierra Nevada Mountains in California.

Still mostly asleep and knowing that she can be overly paranoid, I dismissed the faint noises as nothing out of the ordinary and drifted back into dream land almost immediately.

The next morning, crawling out of the back of the truck, I immediately noticed something amiss: The front passenger door was wide open. It must have been like this all night long . . . That's definitely not good!

A few more steps forward and I noticed the crumbs littering the floor of the vehicle and the lid to our large plastic box of food ajar. Did we really just get ransacked by raccoons in the middle of the night? They made off with a half a bag of cereal and a few packets of Ritz Crackers.

The next evening I was the paranoid one, lying there awake and listening for every little noise. Just before drifting off, I heard the pitter-patter of little feet on the hood of my truck.

The dastardly creatures had returned looking for another easy meal.

Being Footloose

How long could you travel if you were only paying $10–20 per night while staying in some of the most beautiful places on the planet? How about if lodging were absolutely free and your only major expenses were food and gasoline? Imagine waking up beside a serene lake, a chain of snow-covered mountains, or the solitude and vast open space of the desert . . .

Yes, I'm talking about hitting the road and camping beneath the stars, but perhaps not in the way you're thinking. So if you're not a big fan of camping, stay with me for a minute.

From Route 66 to Jack Kerouac, road-tripping is a time-honored American tradition and remains one of the absolute best ways to really get to know a place.

It should not be denied . . . that being footloose has always exhilarated us. It is associated in our minds with escape from history and oppression and law and irksome obligations, with absolute freedom, and the road has always led West.

—Wallace Stegner in *The American West as Living Space*

What I'm referring to here is often known as "overlanding," which differs from a simple road trip in that you are totally self-sufficient with no need for restaurants, hotels, and similarly costly expenses when you are on the go.

The Ultimate Freedom

Traveling overland allows you the freedom to see and go wherever you want, when you want, while not relying on others. You have everything you need within your mode of travel to live a happy and healthy life: food, kitchen, a comfortable place to sleep, and ample entertainment if you enjoy the outdoors (and traditional entertainment as well, thanks to all our electronics).

Overlanding (even though I didn't know that name when I set out) is how I was really introduced to the life of long-term travel. At the beginning of 2013, I set out in my 1991 Toyota 4x4 pickup truck, equipped with a canopy and plywood organizational system in the back. It had around 140,000 miles when I began driving across the frozen flatlands of the North as I made my way to the Rocky Mountains. Over the course of the year, I zigged and zagged my way across the American Southwest, putting another 20,000 or so miles on my truck.

I was able to pursue my passions, experience life on the open road, drive unfamiliar new areas, and I began to like all the days of the week—not just Friday and Saturday. I've traveled in other manners since, but overlanding will probably always remain one of my absolute favorite methods for traveling. The bonus is that it is quite affordable.

Simplicity

Overlanding is not complicated; it essentially just boils down to having a home on wheels, and I don't mean a big ol' expensive, gas-guzzling RV. I've spent many hundreds of nights in total driving and living out of the back of my Toyota pickup, which is a relatively small truck with a standard six-foot long bed and elevated canopy.

It's like taking a Tiny Home to a whole new level.

During that time I've been able to wake up on the

beaches of Mexico, I've slept in the snow of the Canadian Rockies, and I've ventured to many of the most iconic National Parks in the United States. I've done it solo and I've done it with my girlfriend, Andrea (who at the time had done very little camping, but thankfully has come to enjoy the comfort of life from the truck). The freedom of the open road and having everything I need within the canopy has been one of the most freeing and defining journeys of my life.

People do it with dogs, people do it with their children. It is something that is accessible to virtually everyone.

Ease

Many people think of camping as really roughing it. In my experience, nothing could be further from the truth if you are overlanding. We cook big, hearty breakfasts, we eat well, we sleep inside the covered confines of the truck, we've got our comfy camp chairs and even a hammock to string up between trees.

Occasionally we enjoy WiFi at camp, and we regularly watch movies and TV shows on the laptop at night. Overlanding may require a few compromises, but not too many, and in exchange you have total freedom, an ever-changing scenery, and more often than not views that easily beat most upscale hotels.

Trucks are by no means the only option. Plenty of people travel out of vans, smaller cars, or even motorcycles. You aren't even limited to automobiles—it's the same principle whether you are bicycling long distances with camping and cooking gear, or hiking the Appalachian Trail for six months with all your gear on your back.

My buddy, Nate Damm, set off on a massive trek, walking from the Atlantic Ocean all the way to the Pacific in California while seeing the country from a perspective and pace that most will never be able to appreciate. In that time he made amazing connections with strangers all over the country through numerous serendipitous encounters, and all while spending very little money in total.

You aren't even limited to the United States. The annual Overland Expo in Flagstaff, Arizona is full of people who have driven their rigs to the ends of the Earth, from Alaska to Patagonia, from South Africa to Siberia. Your imagination is your limit when you travel as an overlander because continents certainly won't limit you.

It all comes down to being self-sufficient.

Most people are familiar with campgrounds and how they are generally quite affordable and comfortable, but what many may not realize is there are also a huge number of free campsites (check out FreeCampsites.net) that you can take advantage of on public lands across the United States, and in many, many other countries (check out iOverlander.com) as well. Within the States one can generally rely on BLM (Bureau of Land Management) and Forest Service land to offer up ample free camping opportunities with your vehicle.

You've got million dollar views with Mother Nature surrounding you. There really is nothing like it.

Imagine finally visiting all those remarkable places that have inspired generations: the Grand Canyon at sunrise, the last light bouncing off the granite walls of Yosemite Valley, the majestic hoodoos in Bryce Canyon, or the sun-soaked beaches of Baja California. It's all right there, so accessible and so affordable.

It's like that joke that gets passed around on the Internet: a photo of a "five-star hotel" with luxurious accommodation on one side and on the other, a "billion-star hotel" with a tent glowing under the Milky Way.

Wal-Mart: Save Money, Live Better

Having an overland rig allows you to sleep in the comfort of your vehicle and also enables you to save big money while passing between National Parks and other public lands by sleeping in suburban areas like Wal-Mart parking lots (which is actually welcomed and quite common) where you would otherwise have to book a hotel room.

One of my new favorites instead of Wal-Mart parking lots are the now ubiquitous casinos across most of the American West. They typically offer free overnight dry camping, free drinks, cheap entertainment and food, and quite often a little bit of free money to gamble.

It's actually a pretty great resource for those on the road, and it's always a blast to walk away with $10–15 of winnings from their free play promotions, which you can put toward a (now free) dinner or breakfast. You can find a list of casinos that permit overnight camping along with user reviews at CasinoCamper.com.

Your Single Greatest Expense

With the overlanding life, your biggest expense per month will likely be gasoline, but you will pay very little for lodging, so it basically evens out. One of the biggest realizations is that if you travel at a slower pace and stay put to explore an area a little more, you will dramatically reduce your daily expenses. That is to say that if you doubled your trip length and reduced your travel speed by half, you would not double the price of your overall trip.

You could travel 20,000 miles in six months and spend, say $4,000 in gasoline (at 20 MPG and $4 per gallon gas prices), which equates to $666 per month in gasoline, or you could travel that same 20,000 miles over the course of a year ($333 per month in gas), and you would not even come close to doubling your total cost of the trip since gasoline and maintenance are your biggest expenses, while food and lodging remain a much smaller portion of your overall budget.

I have published cost of living reports for my lengthy road trips, and I find that I typically spend between $300 to $600 per month on gasoline in my vehicle with 17 MPG, thus allowing me $600 to $900 for the rest of my living expenses, which isn't hard to stay within. I've done these trips solo at a slower pace and done it as a couple at a more rapid clip. The average costs remain relatively stable at around $1,200 per month per person or less.

Hablo un Poco . . .

Traveling in foreign countries with your vehicle may seem like an intimidating proposition with the added complications of needing tourist visas and potential import paperwork for the vehicle—but all of these things can be taken care of right at the border as you travel. Countless numbers of people have set out on these journeys without even speaking the local language when they started, but you'll get more out of your travels if you pick up a little bit of the local language.

Traveling in another country in this manner is incredibly liberating and differs from the standard manner of travel where you can't get off the beaten path because you must rely on public transportation, hotels and hostels, and constantly eating out. Again, while overlanding, you are self-contained and self-sufficient.

We've recently begun driving through Mexico, and it has been a great experience thus far. I've known others who have driven the length of the Americas (across 17+ countries and all the way to Patagonia, the southernmost tip of South America) over the course of a year for about $70 per day as a couple ($2,100 per month, or $1,050 per person per month).

I began my perpetual travels by living out of the back of my truck, and I saw more within that year of the United States than I feel like I saw of it in all my previous years combined. I couldn't recommend it more.

Bottom Line

In order to take this approach there is a moderate to high barrier to entry, which depends on purchasing and/or outfitting an appropriate vehicle, including basic camping gear. Though you can take on major trips in almost any vehicle, you will be most comfortable in a truck or van.

After getting started, there is very minimal effort—you're just driving around and finding cheap or free places to spend the night, which is quite easy thanks to the

Internet.

Taking this approach allowed me to save a rough estimate of $15 per night by using free campsites (up to $450 per month) versus a normal camping road trip. If you would otherwise be paying for a hotel, the savings are much more dramatic. Not paying for public transportation provides savings, as well as being able to cook for yourself while on the road.

In order to stay within our $1,200 budget for a month, you would be looking at spending no more than $400–600 per month for gasoline (your vehicle is your lodging in this case—be sure to balance paid camping with free options or cover less mileage in a given month), $600–800 in other expenses for food and activities, for an average of $20–30 per day, an easily achievable number if you cook the majority of your meals and spend the bulk of your time in the outdoors.

How to Get Started

Overlanding requires a capable vehicle that is equipped with all that you may need to sleep, cook, and otherwise live comfortably. The two most popular and capable types of vehicles are pickup trucks equipped with a canopy (SUVs can work too) or vans of virtually any style (even mini-vans). Those are by no means the only options: I've known people to travel long term out of their small hatchbacks, Subaru's, or other vehicles.

I'm a big fan of working with what you've got, meaning it's preferable to try and work with the vehicle you already own instead of complicating things and holding out for that perfect overlanding vehicle. Indeed, more often than not, your old reliable vehicle may be preferable to the latest and greatest because it can be repaired by any competent mechanic since parts are normally ubiquitous and it doesn't have the added complication of strange electronic components, and, particularly if you might be interested in driving to another country, an older vehicle doesn't stand out so much.

The imperfect travel vehicle you own beats the perfect vehicle you'll own "someday," every single time.

Trucks and vans both offer a good balance between providing gear storage and livable space. From my perspective, a van has the advantage over trucks by having a greater amount of living space and being more comfortable while a 4WD truck offers better accessibility to more off-the-beaten-path areas.

Generally people will build out their rigs with systems for organization and sleeping. In a truck it can be a simple elevated sleeping platform with gear storage underneath. In a van there is space for an elevated bed and often a mini-kitchen.

There are many overlanders who spend more time, money, and effort outfitting their vehicles and preparing to travel than they actually spend traveling. Meanwhile, there are those who just go with what they've got and make it work for them.

Why Embrace Minimalism?
Speaking of those who over-prep, over-plan, and over-build their rigs, try your hardest to keep things simple.

There are a number of reasons you want to embrace minimalism and simplify when it comes to overlanding:

- The more complicated your build, the more you will spend in time and money to achieve it, and the more you will spend burning gas due to the additional weight. Both of which equal less money to travel.

- Your space is limited, and it really is like taking a Tiny House to the extreme. Everything should be well organized, optimizing the limited space you have, and everything you bring should be something you regularly use—better still if it is multipurpose.

- One of the fringe benefits of long-term travel, no matter what style it is, is that it forces you to exercise minimalism. Whether you travel by backpack, truck, bicycle or boat, you don't want to be wasting valuable space and kicking yourself for bringing it along.

This forced minimalism also makes you really realize how little you need to be happy, healthy, and equipped for a variety of situations. The amount of things you own tends to be directly related to the amount of space you have to fill. Keep it simple, less is more in this situation.

As Yvon Chouinard, the founder of Patagonia gear company, put it: "The hardest thing in the world is to simplify your life. It's so easy to make it complex."

Boiling It Down

It is beyond the scope of this book to speak to everything that a person may need or want for overlanding, but if we boil it down to its simplest elements, you would need:

- A good place to sleep (a warm sleeping bag and comfortable sleeping pad), preferably within the confines of your vehicle, which should open up sleeping options unavailable to those who use a standard tent or vehicle roof top tent.

- Full kitchen, which includes a stove (I use a simple dual burner propane stove), all the standard kitchen supplies from a bowl, plate, utensils, frying pan, spatula, knife, etc. You can utilize things from your standard kitchen, so long as they aren't glass and breakable, and you'll need sufficient water storage (get a large, hard-sided water container between 2.5 to 5 gallons).

- Be sure to pack clothes to cover a variety of climates and temperatures based on where you will travel. You'll most likely need to cover temperatures that range from very hot to fairly cold, no matter where you go. Some ill-informed overlanders are shocked to encounter high, mountainous areas in Mexico with cold nights when they imagined they would only be camped out on the beach.

Yes, you can buy fancy ultralight titanium cookware, quick dry travel towels and clothes, or the latest and greatest overlanding equipment from roof racks and Hi-

Lift jacks to mini-fridges and solar panels. But here's the thing: all of that is nice, but it absolutely isn't necessary. You can get pretty far with the basics mentioned above, along with your passport and vehicle title and registration.

Find Balance

Again, you want to achieve the balance between not bringing too much, bringing most everything you'll need, and trying to ensure a good base level of comfort. You don't need to plan for every absolute contingency. This means a comfortable sleep setup with a real pillow and nice mattress (either a thick foam pad or inflatable air mattress), camp chairs for hanging out, and perhaps a nice hammock. No matter where you go in the world, they sell things to keep you clothed, fed, and your car running.

Don't be afraid to bring a luxury item or two if it is something regularly used and would otherwise make you unhappy to be without. For instance, I brought along my Aeropress in order to make truly amazing coffee while camping. Sure, I could just drink cheap instant coffee, but I don't want to suffer while traveling. You want to ensure that you are comfortable in your overlanding setup, especially if you're in it for the long term.

If you have a comfortable place to sleep and are able to eat well, you've covered the two biggest things to keep you happy and healthy on the road. We alternate between cooking real meals like hearty breakfast burritos (fry some potatoes, season with garlic powder, salt and pepper, toss in some onions, then scramble eggs into the mix—delicious!) with quick and easily prepared foods like simple pasta or rice dishes that are basically add water, heat, then eat.

Remember to Stay Sane

In order to maintain your sanity and enjoy your time on the road, it is also imperative that you aren't in a cycle of drive, sleep, repeat. I find it is best to limit my driving to no more than 3–4 hours per day. This allows time to actually do things—that's the whole reason you're traveling, right? Hiking, climbing, photography, sightseeing, writing, etc.

Again, traveling slower allows you to see and do more while also being much cheaper on the daily budget. Also, be sure to plan where you're going to camp that night, so you're not searching at the last minute in the dark.

That, my friends, is overlanding in a nutshell, and it really is one of the most amazing ways to travel the world.

Q and A

What about showers and personal hygiene?

That's the first time I've ever got that question! I'm kidding. That's probably one of the most common questions and biggest concerns for some people. The truth of the matter is, yes, your daily showering will probably be impacted.

In between showers, you can embrace the baby wipe method . . . Just buy a cheap box of those wet wipes and give yourself a quick clean every day. They are surprisingly effective. Another option is to do a face-arm-and leg wash in a sink, i.e., a "birdbath," which can make you feel quite refreshed.

There are numerous places where you can find pay showers including truck stops, gear stores, public beaches, and some campgrounds that will allow you to pay separately for the shower even if you aren't camped there. You could also just plan to camp at campgrounds like that every few days: RV parks, State Parks, and KOAs are all good places to start. Some of those more expensive camping options also offer WiFi, so you can kill two birds with one stone.

There are other options as well, including solar showers, which are basically large black water bags that you leave in the sun to heat up and which feature a hose and mini showerhead.

I know it can be a shock and adjustment, but you'll do just fine. Andrea had not done much camping at all before we met and is a strict shower-every-day type person. But after hitting the road for months, you just kind of adapt to showering a little less frequently and making do. It's really not a major catastrophe.

Is it safe?

The other major concern that many people have is related to safety. We are bombarded with so much bad news (that's the only kind of news, right?) that we begin to distort reality ourselves.

In my hundreds of nights camping out of the back of my truck, in semi-urban parking lots, casino parking garages in Las Vegas, the middle of absolute nowhere in the States, and even in Mexico (which features a whole new level of fear mongering in US media), I can count on one hand—no, make that one finger—the amount of times where I was ever disturbed by a stranger while sleeping in my truck . . . And it happened way up in the friendly north of Canada.

I'm exaggerating for effect. It was actually just a private security guard waking me up from a deep sleep with a loud knock on my window at 4 a.m. telling me I couldn't camp there. It was my fault too because they had signs posted saying, "No overnight parking," but I didn't think it was actually enforced, especially in November with snow and ice covering everything after a big storm.

I don't even lock the back canopy when I am sleeping inside (I actually don't have the ability to do so—though you could fashion up a simple DIY lock). Some recommend that you should always be able to quickly and easily access your driver's seat and even leave the key in the ignition (too paranoid, I think). Vans probably have the best layout for security purposes in this respect whereas in a truck you have no access to the cab from the truck bed.

I think overlanding or camping in your vehicle is at least as safe as tent camping (which is very safe), if not more so. The only key difference is perhaps spending more nights in urban and suburban areas (I always prefer suburban).

Do I need to be mechanically inclined?

I am decidedly not mechanically inclined though I continue to learn more the longer I am on the road. I have unfortunately had problems while I've been on the road, the worst of which was when my timing chain broke as I was leaving Bryce Canyon National Park, leaving me stranded on the side of the road with a very weak cell signal. A few days earlier I had been deep into Grand Staircase Escalante National Monument, down a long dirt road, which would have been a much worse place to break down.

Thankfully I had a AAA membership and was able to get a call through (despite it being dropped a few times). I got a tow to the closest big city, which meant making small talk with the driver for well over an hour to get to Cedar City. The repairs ended up costing me over $1,000 (what I would normally spend in a month on the road), and I was stuck in town for two nights.

I've also gotten a flat in the middle of nowhere Colorado. I had never changed a tire on my truck before that, but I figured it out, and a stranger even stopped to let me use his far superior lug wrench when he saw me struggling with mine.

This is all to say that no, you need not be a mechanical whiz (though you can certainly leave with more confidence if you are), but at the least I would recommend that you learn the bare minimum of car maintenance (regular checks of oil and fluids) and that you go read the *Auto Repair for Dummies* book. I traveled with a small set of tools that included screwdrivers, pliers, wrench, socket wrench, duct tape, zip ties, etc. Even if you don't know anything about engines (like me), at least familiarize yourself with the parts and get in the habit of regularly (at least once a week) taking a look under the hood, checking the fluid levels, air filter, and ensure that everything "looks good."

Deeann's Story

Deeann Davis connected with me initially via my private Facebook truck camping group. Deeann has been out there truck camping and overlanding for a while now. I loved her story and asked her to share her perspective as an experienced female truck camper. Here's Deeann's story:

I've been truck camping since about 1997, almost 20 years ago. I had a truck with a Leer Camper shell on it and I was talking to a friend at work and I just blurted out: "You know, I should build a bed in the back of my truck to sleep in so that I could travel. I could stow all my gear in totes under the bed. That would be an easy and fast way to travel. Would you like to come with me?" And she said: "Yeah. That would be cool." So, that's what we did.

I came up with my own design for the bed in the back and did all the work myself. I've worked in maintenance all my life, so I knew how to do all that kind of thing. It was easy to do. It took about a month in all to get it ready and equipped. Then we were ready to fly down the road. And fly we did. We traveled everywhere we could think of.

When I'm away from home, my truck becomes my new home. It's the vehicle that opens up new adventures for me. This truck took me to Moab, Utah, and I discovered Dead Horse State Park where Thelma and Louise took the plunge. It took me to California where I stood in awe of the giant redwoods. It took me to Glacier National Park where I had to stop to let a grizzly walk down the road ahead of me. Oh, this old truck of mine . . . her heart beats in step to mine.

Do I love truck camping? Oh, yeah. You can do it anywhere that there's enough space for your truck. Don't stick me in a motel. I want to sit around a campfire at night and see the moon and the stars. I want to hear the sounds of nature all around me. Yep, just give me enough space to park my truck.

Sometimes people ask me if it scares me to travel (being a woman). I'd have to say that I'm not afraid. I had a scary feeling one time up in the mountains and got up in the night and left the camp area. I had a bad feeling the minute we pulled into this area. It was too isolated and overgrown—tall grass, shrubs, and trees everywhere. And we were in grizzly territory. It unnerved me to think that a bear could be very close to us lurking in the greenery and we couldn't see it. I tried to shake off the feeling.

I asked my travel partner about it, and she wasn't bothered by it at all. So I let it go. When the sun finally went down I became very agitated and nervous. My partner began to feel the same way. The longer we lay in bed, the stronger the unease became. So we got up, jumped in the truck, and drove into town. We ended up sleeping in a motel parking lot. To this day I can't say that we were actually in any kind of danger, but I became a firm believer in listening to my intuition. If you don't feel safe, just leave the area. Listen to what your inner being is telling you. And always remember to be cautious of your surroundings. Enjoy your trip but use common sense as you travel.

This is a beautiful country that we live in. There's a wonderful diversity of nature, terrain, and culture just down the road. I can't think of a better way to see it and experience it firsthand. Living out of the back of my truck appeals to my inner nature to be one with the land, to forego the creature comforts of my house and discover new ways to enjoy the beauty of the world around me.

Big Chapter, Small Summary

- Overlanding is one of the most freeing ways to travel, whether domestically or internationally.

- It isn't really complicated; indeed simple is better: just have a nice place to sleep and a cooking and kitchen setup.
- Truck camping or van-life is not solely for young people—I have met and heard from dozens of people of all stripes: older retirees, solo females, couples, etc.

Benefits

- *Spontaneity*

Of all the forms of travel I've embarked on, I have never felt so free as when I'm traveling as an overlander. Again, you are completely self-contained and can travel when and where you please. You have total flexibility to follow the weather, head to a nice campground, venture way off the grid down a long dirt road, or spend some time in the city.

- *Striking a Balance between Moving Too Slow or Too Fast*

Slow travel is definitely one of the keys to more affordable travel, at least on a cost per day basis. You could hike along the Pacific Crest Trail or bicycle down the West Coast very affordably because you aren't expending gas. But for many people that is a form of travel that is either too slow or too physically demanding. Obviously, you could also just fly from San Diego to Seattle and "see" the West Coast, but that isn't really seeing anything at all. Travel by automobile allows you to move slowly or to cover a great deal of ground. It is the perfect balance between the two.

- *Self-Sufficiency*

This is the most important aspect of overland travel, and you lose the primary benefit if you have to rely on hotels or restaurants while traveling. Being able to cook and sleep comfortably in your vehicle opens up almost unlimited possibilities. Don't listen to that *Saturday Night Live* skit with Chris Farley talking about how bad it is to live in a van down by the river . . .

Drawbacks

- *Potential for Mechanical Problems*

This is always the biggest concern with a major road trip, particularly if your vehicle is a little older (mine is a 1991). When something does go wrong with your vehicle, it is always very expensive and can put a big dent in your travel budget. This is just something you'll have to accept as a risk with this manner of travel. In the United States, I would also advise that you purchase AAA Premier membership, which offers tows for up to 200 miles. Things may go wrong, but that is all part of the adventure and could just as easily happen one day while driving to work.

- *Weather*

While you do have the flexibility to keep heading to where the weather is good, you will unavoidably have to deal with inclement weather at some point. This could mean rain, snow, or unrelenting heat. I have dealt with them all, and rain is certainly my least favorite. Having a simple awning over the entryway of the canopy helps a great deal (a cheap tarp) along with a few good books on your Kindle. If the weather just won't cooperate that day and there is nowhere nearby where I can escape to better conditions, I will usually just spend the day at a local coffee shop.

- *Personal Space*

You will be living within a confined space, which may get to you at some point, either due to weather as mentioned above or illness (like when I got sick in Death Valley). If you're traveling with another person, it will put your relationship to the test at times being together all day, every day.

- *Getting Outfitted*

You will need a decent vehicle, a simple organizational system, as well as the basic amount of gear to cook, sleep, and be comfortable. I've had my truck forever, but I had to buy a canopy ($1,000+), build storage and organization with plywood ($100), and buy the related camping gear (much of which I already had on hand, but you can expect to spend another few hundred dollars). I would highly recommend buying your gear from REI.com as they have an extremely generous return policy for members of their co-op. When one air mattress sprung a leak two months later, they replaced it with no questions asked. But once you've invested the time and money to get your rig equipped, you are essentially good to go.

Resources and Further Reading

- Blog Post: Ultimate Guide to Truck Camping

I'm a big fan of truck camping, so if you have a truck and want to find out how to best outfit your rig, be sure to check out my detailed blog post, the Ultimate Guide to Truck Camping, along with my numerous YouTube videos with tips and tricks.

- Book: *Vanabode by Jason Odom*

VanLife remains one of the most popular and comfortable ways to live long term out of a vehicle. You should definitely take a look at the Vanabode website and ebook, it is the most detailed resource on this subject that I have seen. Much of the information applies equally well to any long-term traveler who will be vehicle-based, whether or not it is a van.

- Website: Life Remotely – liferemotely.com

If you're at all interested in driving overland through Central and South America, you absolutely must read the *Life Remotely* book—they go into painstaking detail about budgets and logistics from their travels and are one of the reasons why I had the confidence to set out myself on this journey south of the border.

- Website: Expedition Portal – expeditionportal.com

Expedition Portal remains one of the greatest resources for all manner of overland travelers and contains a wealth of information within the forum section.

- Book: *Life on Foot by Nate Damm*

Nate Damm, my buddy who walked across America, has a most excellent book about his journey titled *Life on Foot*. Be sure to check it out.

For links to all the resources and materials mentioned in this chapter, be sure to visit:

www.desktodirtbag.com/bigtravel-paperback

CHAPTER 4

FLY FOR FREE

A Day at the Beach

"No problem!" the moto taxi driver shouted in Arabic over the roar of the motorcycle engine as he pulled the bottom of his t-shirt up over his face to protect his eyes.

We'd just ridden two hours along the sandy beaches and lapping waves of the Red Sea to arrive in Mocha, Yemen, one of the world's original coffee ports . . . only to be greeted by this most unpleasant sight.

Concernedly I clutched onto the back of the seat a little tighter as we road full bore into the sandstorm, completely unprotected from the elements.

A thick, swirling brown torrent of sand blasted us as we continued motoring into this small port city. It was like something I'd seen in the movies.

The driver continued along without pause, peering carefully through the thin fabric of his shirt with his belly hanging out below. The sand hung in the air over the salty sea as we arrived at this seemingly famous town after drinking so many delicious mochas, yet in reality it is nearly completely unknown.

I had sand in my eyes, ears, covering me all over, as well as inside my clothes. It was a long trip to get to Mocha, but after a quick lunch of fresh fish, I hopped into a regular taxi and this time headed inland. I'd had enough sand for the day.

Jet-Setting

In the last chapter we talked about the merits of going overland, but there's just nothing quite like jetting off to the other side of the world in a day. Domestic flights are pretty affordable, but once you start looking to travel to new continents, the prices can be prohibitively expensive. Thankfully one of the easiest ways to save significant money while traveling is also one of the most rewarding.

Would you like to jet off to some far-flung international destination for free? Maybe that dream trip to Patagonia, Australia, or India doesn't sound feasible with flights over $1,000 . . . Well, for very little time and not much extra effort, you can get that same flight basically free—though you still have to pay some fees and taxes.

Note: This is only available to those of you from the United States. Sorry, if you're from elsewhere, you'll want to skip this chapter—don't worry, the next two tactics still apply!

Steve Kamb of Nerd Fitness picked up a "round the world" ticket (four continents, nine countries) for only $418. Chris Guillebeau used the approach in his quest to visit every country in the world over the course of 10+ years.

Your goals may be decidedly less ambitious, but it is no less rewarding to save hundreds, or even thousands, of dollars on your flights.

Credit Card Based Travel Hacking

I got into travel hacking a few years back, which, if you're not familiar, is not as nefarious as it sounds and is essentially just finding ways to maximize your ability to earn and redeem airline miles through frequent flyer programs, most often through credit card based travel hacking opportunities.

This is one you can and should do whether you've got a trip in the works or not. Even if you are planning a lengthy overlanding trip and don't anticipate flying, I'd still get on board with this one, as you never know when it might come in handy to book a free flight. Perhaps for an emergency trip back home while on the road, or maybe you'll want a vacation from your long-term travels? I've been there, and once you start traveling like this, you'll know what I mean. Or you can just hang on to the miles for future travels . . .

By taking advantage of credit card travel hacking I have already saved about $1,400 in cash on booked flights, both internationally and domestically. I'm not a hardcore mileage hacker at all, but I do it casually when good opportunities present themselves because it is so easy to do and requires little extra effort.

Using these same principles, my cousin just returned from a family vacation to Hawaii for the five of them (the parents and three kids) for just $55 round trip. That's $55 for everyone, not per person. You can imagine how much that would've cost to book outright . . . at least $500 per ticket.

While I was living in Medellin, Colombia, my mom was able to come down for a short visit (I'm sure she never in her wildest dreams imagined she would go to Colombia) by using her frequent flier miles, which only ended up costing her $104.50 in taxes and 47,500 miles for a round trip flight.

I've talked to other friends and family about doing this, and some of have just dismissed the opportunity outright. I honestly cannot understand why anyone wouldn't want to take advantage of the opportunity to fly for practically free instead of paying sticker price for an airline ticket. It's a no-brainer!

It reminds me of that *Breaking Bad* scene where the waitress in Denny's is trying to prod Walt into his free birthday breakfast: "Even if I was like rich, free's always good!"

A few years ago, I purchased the Frequent Flyer Master guide from *Unconventional Guides*, which really set me off down this direction. The man behind *Unconventional Guides*, Chris Guillebeau, took travel hacking to the extreme as he used the process to collect millions of miles on his quest to visit every country in the world.

People like Chris obviously really work the system to collect such a huge amount of miles, but you can take a much more casual approach like I did and still see big results.

Following his guide and the lessons within, I started hacking the system immediately and easily accrued a few hundred thousand miles with very little extra work or effort.

It was really cool.

Minus $700+

My first big award redemption came around Christmas one year. I procrastinated on buying a ticket home for the holidays because my work schedule wasn't clear (that's how Congress works—leave everything until the last minute).

By the time we were finally somewhat clear on dates and I was able to purchase the ticket, it was only about two weeks before Christmas, and by that time the prices had climbed to around $800 round trip to fly back home to Seattle from the East Coast.

Ouch.

I ended up shelling out 50,000 miles (still kind of expensive) with American Airlines and just $85 cash for the taxes and fees. Much better.

It was my first time saving $700+ on a flight. Pretty cool! It completely transformed my idea of travel not being affordable and got the wheels turning for the future.

I was happy to save $700+ that first time around—but I was a little disappointed after the fact because I could have easily put those miles toward redeeming a much more expensive international flight to, say, Buenos Aires for just a handful more miles, which would otherwise easily cost $1,200+ out of pocket.

At the time of writing this, I've got about 150,000 miles on hand which is equivalent to two (or more) round trip international flights anywhere in the world, or about five round trip domestic flights. That is a ton of money that I can save on future flights, even though I don't have any immediate plans to fly.

It offers one of the biggest returns for the least amount of work and can be done by most anyone. It is a Big Win, as personal finance blogger Ramit Sethi would put it, and for many people, those Big Wins provide a bigger psychological boost of success than the little wins, which will help keep you going in your pursuit of long-term travel.

Mileage hacking is only to be used by those with good credit, no ongoing problems struggling with debt, and who don't have any problem paying off their credit cards in full every month.

There are many other worthwhile offers to pursue beyond the airline mileage cards, including some that provide straight cash bonuses or hotel loyalty credit cards that offer up to a week of free stays in top-of-the-line resorts anywhere in the world. You can easily do both airline cards and hotel cards. Why not?

Mileage hacking and credit cards are how I got started in this world of travel hacking, even back while I was still working the desk job. It is extremely rewarding and provides the slippery slope you need to embrace a travel hacker's perspective in all your future travels.

Bottom Line

In order to take this approach, the barrier to entry is almost non-existent, just a good credit score and identifying opportunities. Also, it is likely one of the easiest ways to start saving big money to travel.

After getting started, there is moderate effort if you must meet a minimum spend requirement, but very minimal effort in order to redeem miles.

Taking this approach allowed me to save $700 on two flights. You can save even more. Remember—it is best to use mileage on expensive international flights rather than domestic flights.

In order to stay within our $1,200 budget for a month, you would need to look at more affordable international destinations where the dollar goes further. Flying for free to an international destination leaves you with $1,200 to spend in lodging and activities. Budget travelers can find lodging for $20 or less per night ($500 per month), leaving you with $700, or $23 per day, for food and activities—an easily achievable number in many parts of the world.

How to Get Started

The first and most important step is to find a current promotional credit card offer. Offers are constantly changing, so it is no use to mention specific promotions in this book and point you to an offer that has already expired. I'd just recommend you visit CardsforTravel.com, which is regularly updated to highlight the current best offers available.

Credit card bonuses range from cold hard cash (I've signed up for cards to simply get $300, which I actually used part of to start my blog) to 50,000 or even 75,000 in airline frequent flier miles—the latter of which is enough for a round trip flight almost anywhere in the world.

Anything over 50,000 miles is an offer that is definitely worth taking a closer look at. I don't generally bother with anything less than 40,000 miles (though that is still enough for a round trip domestic flight or one-way international flight). When I got started, I picked up two separate credit cards for American Airlines, which netted me bonuses of 75,000 each . . . 150,000 frequent flier miles can take you a really long way.

Once you've found an appealing card online, make sure to analyze the details about what requirements you will need to meet in order to receive the miles and how difficult that may or may not be for you.

More often than not you will need to meet some minimum requirements in order to receive the mileage bonuses, typically it is meeting a certain level of spending within a limited amount of time—for instance $3,000 dollars within three months. I've got more about tricky ways to meet minimum spend requirements in a moment. And typically these cards carry an annual fee of $70–90 per year that is waived the first year for new customers.

Promotions do vary though, and some can be extremely easy to fulfill. I recently received 50,000 miles for signing up for a card with a $89 annual fee (not waived), but which awarded the miles with the first purchase of anything (I just bought a drink from Starbucks). An amazing deal that is much easier to achieve than minimum spend cards, and in the future I'll get a flight or two out of it for a measly $89 investment.

After you've identified and applied for an awesome new credit card, be sure to create your frequent flier account with the corresponding airline if you don't have one already. This step is free and easy.

It is easiest to get started with credit card offers before you start traveling, but once you hit the road, you can still apply for appealing offers if you utilize the mailing address of your parents or a trusted friend. While traveling, it is great to maintain a "home base" where you can receive correspondence such as this. With the help of your person on the ground, you can have them forward it on to you wherever you may be currently traveling or just retain the card number and security code from the back of the card in your records, call to activate the card, then have them cut up the card (which you can then use for online bill pay or shopping).

Don't be a Sucker

Credit card companies go to big lengths to bring on new customers and will pay big bucks to acquire them because they know that the average American has a huge problem with credit cards, will carry a balance, and will make them loads of money down the road on interest rates and fees.

Don't be fooled—these mileage bonuses aren't out of the kindness of their hearts; they are hoping to make their money back. Your money. But if you are smart and do it right, you will come out ahead with hundreds of dollars worth of airline frequent flier miles without spending a single cent more than you already would have.

The trick (it isn't really a trick) is to just be responsible with your cards, pay them off in full every month, and make them actually work for you, instead of against you.

The best thing you can do to ensure you don't mess up is to immediately login to your new credit card and set the card to automatically pay the balance in full each month when due.

No missing payments, no late fees, no interest charges. No excuses.

Autopay is your friend and will ensure that you come out ahead against the credit card companies.

Meet the Minimum Spend

So you found the best bonuses currently available, signed up for the credit card, and now you need to meet the minimum spend within a certain period of time, we'll go with the pretty common example of $3,000 in three months.

But you may be wondering, "Now how do I manage to spend $3,000 within three months, Ryan?" Great question. Three thousand dollars is a lot of money. But it is important to remember that we are only talking about charges on the card and not an extra $3,000 of out-of-pocket expenses.

First and foremost, put all of your regular spending on the card—from your groceries to your gas to your cell phone bill. Everything.

Second, if you have any big purchases pending in the near future, plan your credit card applications around that. Another obvious tactic is to just volunteer to put some large expenses of good friends or family on your card to help you reach the minimum spend and have them pay you back with cash or check.

Third, you can also meet the minimum spend requirement by spending money without really spending money, which is known as "manufactured" spending.

Manufactured Spending

What I mean by that is there are a few nifty tricks out there where you can meet your minimum spend requirement for credit cards without actually kissing that money goodbye. You're essentially just moving money around for little to no cost in order to get those miles.

For example you can purchase Visa gift cards, which are as good as cash and can be spent in the future. You just need to buy enough to make up the difference between your regular spending (point one above) and your minimum spend requirement.

You can loan out money on Kiva.org, a microlending service (it is a loan to be paid back), and help a budding entrepreneur overseas while also helping to meet your minimum spend.

The specific tactics for manufactured spending frequently change, but the strategy remains the same: Spend money without spending it. In the past, people have purchased coins through the US Mint or sent money to friends and family at no charge through the now defunct Amazon Payments. You can browse through the many frequent flier boards and websites for the current preferred method of manufactured spending: FlyerTalk.com, ThePointsGuy.com, or join a membership site like the Travel Hacking Cartel.

Once you've met the minimum requirements of the card promotion, the miles will be posted to your account within a few weeks. Congratulations! In total the process will take a couple months, which is why I recommend that you get started sooner rather than later.

The Cancel Option

If the card has an annual fee (which is usually waived the first year), be sure to put a note on your online calendar for 11 months later to call the credit card company to cancel the card before that year is up, or better yet, you can give them a call and have them downgrade the card to one with no annual fee, thus keeping that line of credit open and not negatively impacting your credit card score as much.

Often when you call and speak to them, they will offer to waive your annual fee for the second year. They've spent a lot of money to gain you as a customer, and they don't want to lose you. You can decide whether to keep the card open in that case, or not—but if you do keep it open, put another note on your calendar for 11 months later.

Just to clarify, once the miles have posted to your account, you are no longer beholden to the credit card company. The miles are yours to keep and have already posted to your frequent flier account, which is separate.

I cancel or downgrade all cards with an annual fee before the year is up. These airline credit cards do offer other fringe benefits, such as free bag check or priority boarding, that you will then lose upon cancellation. I only hold onto one card that has an annual fee, from Alaska Airlines, and that is just because it is the primary carrier in Seattle.

Keeping Track

To keep yourself organized and on top of the dates for

minimum spend and card cancellation, I would recommend Google Calendar (free), which allows you to quickly and easily create reminders that will alert you via the smartphone app, as well as by email.

To keep track of your credit cards and how much you've spent toward your minimum spend, I highly recommend Mint.com, a free service that helps you stay on top of all your accounts (savings, checking, credit cards, investments). Tracking your income and expenses and truly understanding where your money is going every month is also the best way to help you meet your financial objectives, reduce spending where possible when it doesn't serve your travel goals, and identify problems before they escalate (either in unexpected fees and charges, or identifying areas where you spend too much).

I've been using Mint.com for years, and I truly credit it with helping me get a grip on my money and not waste it on things that are unimportant to me.

Like Mint.com for personal finance, there are also a number of websites to help you keep track of all your points and miles across a variety of accounts. I use AwardWallet.com to help me stay on top of all my rewards accounts. I also really appreciate the email notifications when the miles have posted to my account.

Use 'Em—Don't Lose 'Em

The last, and most important, step is to use your miles on an upcoming trip. Remember these miles are to be used, not to hold onto forever for "someday." Miles can lose efficacy over time and succumb to inflation just like real money (that's when your grandma says, "Back in my day, we could buy a loaf of bread for 50 cents!"), so if you wait years to use them, you may find you can't travel quite as far.

Reward flights, including flights on partner airlines, can be redeemed easily through each airline's frequent flier dashboard. Some airlines do not feature all possible partner airline bookings and may require you to call in and speak with a human, but that is the exception, not the rule.

Just like booking tickets and paying with real money, you can find cheaper mileage flights if you have some flexibility in your arrival and departure dates. Be sure to display the rewards calendar and identify cheaper options that may allow you to spend less miles and get another flight later.

The Best Value for Your Miles

Many people calculate the value of their mileage redemption based on cents per mile (CPM). If a plane ticket is currently selling for $800 or can be had for 50,000 frequent flier miles, you would divide 800 by 50,000 to find the CPM, which in this case would be 0.016 or 1.6 cents per mile.

The higher the cents per mile, the better value you are getting for your mile redemption instead of paying cash.

While there is no hard and fast rule about what the ratio should be, many people suggest that anything around 1 cent per mile is better to just purchase outright with cash, while above 1.5 cents per mile provides a good value.

My first award redemption, that last minute flight home for Christmas, was 1.6 cents per mile. So it wasn't the greatest value per mile, but it was still a good deal and most importantly saved me around $700 in expenses.

Miles are almost always better used for international ticket purchases rather than domestic, but it can be helpful to calculate the CPM for a more accurate picture.

As another example of CPM, when I flew to Cartagena, Colombia, I was able to get a one-way ticket for just $346.20. A normal award redemption from North America to South America would typically cost around 30,000 miles on American or Alaska (where most of my miles are).

The CPM on that trip would have been just 1.1 cents per mile and would clearly not have been the best use of my miles. I, therefore, opted to just purchase the ticket outright and save the miles for a future trip.

I was able to score a one-way flight home to Seattle

from Medellin, Colombia for 35,000 miles (again, around Christmas time) and only $95.10 in taxes and fees. The same one-way flight was going for $782 if purchased outright, making it 2.2 CPM, by far the best value of all the examples we've looked at thus far.

And I just saved $686.90 . . . for the second time! Feels pretty good.

Q and A

Am I only limited to flights with the airline where I earned my promotion miles?

No, this is something that many people unfamiliar with frequent flier miles misunderstand. If you have miles with Alaska Airlines, you are not solely limited to the cities where Alaska Airlines directly flies.

My mom traveled from Seattle to Medellin, round trip, for 47,500 miles with her Alaska Air miles, and they definitely don't fly all the way to South America.

All airlines belong to a network of partner airlines, both foreign and domestic. Alaska, for example, is partnered with British Airways, Emirates, Korean Air, Qantas, Delta, American, and a number of others.

There are a few major networks of airlines, and the casual travel hacker probably doesn't need to dig in too much, just search for the partner airlines of the card you are looking to apply for and make sure you can get to the part of the world you want to go to.

It is important to note that miles are not transferable between frequent flier mileage programs, so while Alaska and American are part of the same network, you cannot combine 10,000 miles from Alaska with 30,000 from American to get that 40,000 mile reward ticket. It is far better to have lots of miles in one or two carriers than having miles spread across many different carriers.

Do I have to have a good credit score?

Yes, you do have to have a good credit score (typically

700 or higher) to take advantage of travel hacking like this. If you have a bad score, you probably have had enough financial problems and shouldn't be taking on another credit card anyway. Get your financial house in order, rebuild your credit, and then give it a shot. You can still apply the other lessons in this book.

Do I have to play the credit card game to get free flights?

No, but credit cards are the fastest and easiest way to rack up major miles. Other popular ways to get miles include shopping online through the airline portals where you can get 5x, 7x or even 20x bonuses for every dollar you spend with popular online merchants.

If you are going to do any shopping, you should definitely consider doing it online and check out your mileage program to see if you can get the product along with a free mileage bonus by using their shopping portal.

For instance, with American Airlines I can shop with Backcountry.com, a popular outlet for outdoor gear, and get 7 miles per dollar. If I'm buying a $300 sleeping bag, I'd rake in 2,100 miles just for shopping through the airline portal.

Pretty good for something that doesn't cost you anything but 30 seconds more of your time.

You can even double-dip for miles . . . Go through the shopping portal and buy an e-gift card while getting the points bonus above. Then go back in and use that gift card to purchase what you needed while getting the points bonus a second time. You've effectively doubled your points for a little extra work.

Websites like Rocketmiles.com provide bonuses of up to a few thousand miles per standard hotel booking, which can certainly add up over time. You only need about 12,500 miles for a free one-way ticket in the US.

There are also dining programs that result in 3x or 5x bonuses per dollar when you dine at participating restaurants and use your linked card. Always great to get miles for expenses you were already going to make, and even better when you get a surprise bonus that you didn't even realize you were going to get. Just be sure to register for the dining program in advance.

There are many, many other strategies for earning points—check the resources section for more.

What fees are associated with these cards and "free" flights?

Many of the most valuable airline mileage cards have annual fees associated with them, but almost always those fees are waived for the first year. Just be sure to cancel or downgrade the card before the year is up. And, depending on the bonus and fee, it can still be worth the annual fee if you will be getting a free flight out of the deal, like when I paid the $89 annual fee upfront for 50,000 miles.

When you redeem your miles, you will have to pay taxes and fees, which will vary depending on the exact nature and destination of your flight but, in my experience, have amounted to around $90, which is a pretty modest sum to pay for a flight. The taxes and fees vary by individual airport and country, but are usually much cheaper domestically, which is how my cousin took her whole family to Hawaii for just $55 (about $5 per one-way ticket, per person).

Will it hurt my credit card score?

No. At least not significantly. This has been debunked by many others who are far more aggressive with their credit card applications and churning cards (canceling and reapplying to get the bonus again).

It may take a very small hit in the short term (as any credit inquiry will), but it will benefit in the long run because you have actually increased your total available credit (across all of your cards) while simultaneously utilizing less of that total credit available.

It is bad to fully max out your available credit. If you only have $2,000 in credit available between your cards and they are fully maxed out, your score will reflect that. It is obviously better for your credit score to have $20,000 credit available between all your cards and not carry a balance by paying them off every month.

If you're using your credit cards responsibly, you'll be just fine.

I've got more credit cards (at least two dozen) than any of my immediate friends or family members but my score is right up there in the top tier. The only difference is I get some free flights and they don't.

Katie's Story

Katie Benedetto Jones is a friend that I met at the annual World Domination Summit (also put on by Chris Guillebeau), which is a conference that aims to connect and inspire people living somewhat unconventional lives. I saw that she just booked an amazing trip thanks to travel hacking, so I asked her if she'd be willing to share the details. Here's Katie's story:

I just booked two separate major trips, the first of which is an upcoming tour of Europe across six cities stretching between Madrid and Zurich, which cost me only $271 out of pocket.

The second trip will take me around the world and through 12 cities between Europe, the Middle East, India, and Eastern Asia. The total cost out of pocket was just $317.25.

For less than $600 (in taxes and fees for each stop on the trip), I will get to travel across Europe for a few weeks and later around the world over the course of a month.

The booking is actually three separate trips and only cost 40,000 miles for the European tour (through American Airlines), and 82,500 miles for the world tour (40,000 on American and 42,500 with United—two independent trips).

My initial plan was to try to use these miles to get two trips—one to India and one to Spain. Working with the flight booking service FlightFox, I was able to turn these otherwise straightforward trips into something truly incredible. For instance, I didn't know that you could get up to three 24-hour layovers on each hop—so what started out as a simple trip to India turned into something like a world tour! The Spain trip turned into something more adventurous, too.

You can also use "open-jaw" flights whereby you fly into one city and fly out of another, creating a gap in your travel that you can fill by other means—traveling by train or bus for example. I left an open-jaw between Prague and Istanbul where I will then continue flying on to India.

Using stopovers and open-jaw segments, you can visit more places for the same price in frequent flier miles. Why see one country when you can see a few?

If you've got the airline miles but don't have the knowledge and experience in booking more complicated flights, you can use a service like FlightFox to do some pretty amazing things. In total for booking these three separate trips they charged me $120. Well worth the price!

In reality, I really hate credit cards. The first time I tried travel hacking, I'd been used to using a debit card for everything, so I started to be afraid of my finances for the first time in my life. I tried travel hacking again in order to get these trips, and this time I paid off my credit card immediately, which helped a bunch.

With credit card travel hacking I found that it was quite easy to meet the minimum spend requirements, but a little difficult to have confidence that the miles would come through. The miles my offer included were never listed online, I had to call and ask about them—sometimes to people who would give me wrong information (like the American Airlines guy who told me my offer was only 30,000 miles, until I asked to speak to his supervisor). So that was frustrating—and it takes a long time for the miles to come in, so be sure to start really early—though the frustration is worth it when you book a sweet trip like this!

Also, it's good to know that you need to complete your requirements a few days before the end of the time limit. I forgot that it takes 24–48 hours (or more sometimes) for companies to place the charge on your card, and if the charge isn't placed, it doesn't count, so I was rushing around 24 hours ahead of time buying $100 items at several different places, hoping that one would go through in time. Two did, and one didn't, so I was cutting it far too close.

As long as you're responsible with the card and making sure you get the offer due to you (next time around, I'd keep the promotional paperwork as well, in case there's a problem), I think travel hacking is really awesome. I can't believe the world tour I'm getting to go on here!

Big Chapter, Small Summary

- Credit card travel hacking is one of the easiest ways to start saving big money on your travels.
- You can take a casual approach to credit card travel hacking and still see big rewards.
- You can also redeem your tickets for simple conventional flights or bookings that are quite complex and provide an even greater value.

Benefits

- *Flying for Almost Free*

Do I really need to say any more?

- *First Class and Five-Star*

You can also fly first class and stay in four- or five-star properties by redeeming for slightly more miles or points. I personally don't choose to pay more miles in order to fly first class, but it is the best way to fly first class (except for when someone else is paying for it) because those seats are significantly more expensive than coach when paying cash but only marginally more-so when using miles.

- *Flexibility*

Much more flexibility in terms of when and where you can fly. Unlike the prices of airline tickets, which can fluctuate by hundreds of dollars depending on when you booked it, mileage reward redemptions are much more stable. You can book flights at the last minute for a standard mileage redemption rate. That is to say that prices in miles do vary depending on the day of the flight (i.e., weekends or holidays), but the prices aren't increasing or decreasing on a daily basis, as you find when you pay in cash.

Drawbacks

- *Responsible and Organized*

You must be financially responsible (is that actually a drawback?) and organized. Don't let yourself slip with your payments as you try to meet minimum spends; simply setup your card to pay the balance in full each month on the due date. Be sure to note when to call or downgrade a card with an annual fee (which was probably waived the first year) on an online calendar.

- *Green with Envy*

Making family and friends jealous when you tell them how cheap your flight was. What other downsides could there be to flying for pennies on the dollar?

The 80/20 Approach

You can get started today using all the info contained in this chapter to rack up major miles and get your first free flight(s). Visit CardsforTravel.com, browse through the current best offers, and make it happen.

I'm a follower of the 80/20 approach, which dictates that 80% of our results come from 20% of our efforts. Thanks to this 101 course, you've got all the info you need to take advantage of credit card hacking and get that Big Win that provides 80% of the results with very little effort.

But if you're looking to go beyond that 80% and want

more tactics and details, I'd highly recommend Unconventional Guides' *Frequent Flyer Master* for the 201 level course, which dives more into the nitty gritty, specific ins and outs of particular airline networks, and provides much greater detail about ways to earn miles and get the greatest redemptions, including much more complicated redemptions (round-the-world tickets, open jaw, etc).

If you'd love to travel to more far-flung destinations or just want to save big bucks on the travel that you already are expecting to do (or maybe have to do), then I cannot recommend strongly enough that you get started travel hacking as soon as possible.

It is an extremely rewarding and awesome experience to pay pennies on the dollar for your flights (especially for international flights).

I mean, just think, you could save $700+ on an international flight to a far-flung destination with a low cost of living and use that $700 that you would have spent to cover your living expenses for two weeks or even a month, effectively giving you a half-price vacation.

Resources and Further Reading

- Website: Cards for Travel – cardsfortravel.com

Cards for Travel is a continuously updated resource of the best credit card promotions currently available, whether they are for airline miles or hotel rewards. Check here first for the latest and greatest.

- Blog Post: My Free Flights

More details about the free flights I've managed to take, screen shots of prices and award redemptions and more.

- Book: *Frequent Flyer Master*

This is the awesome guidebook from Unconventional Guides that got me started down this path to free travel. It provides an even greater level of detail about what we've covered here.

- Website: *Flyer Talk – flyertalk.com*

This is a major source of news and forum discussions related to miles, points, and travel hacking.

- Website: *The Points Guy – thepointsguy.com*

This is another major source to turn to when looking for discussions and news in the world of miles and frequent flyer programs.

- Book: *Upgrade Unlocked*

This is the most comprehensive guide on how to travel in luxury without actually spending the money by utilizing these travel hacking principles. Ever wanted to fly first class? It's much better when it is free. Stay in five-star hotels? Again, way better when you don't pay for it.

- Book: *Nomadic Matt's Travel Hacking Guide*

Matt Kepnes is a veteran of the travel blog world and also has an extremely detailed guide available for those wishing to delve beyond the basics. I've gotten a lot of value from his guide as well.

- Website: Flight Fox – flightfox.com

You needn't be an expert to book the more complex reward tickets like those round the world flights—you can utilize services such as FlightFox to do the heavy lifting for a modest fee (you're still saving hundreds or even thousands of dollars in the end).

For links to all the resources and materials mentioned in this chapter, be sure to visit:

www.desktodirtbag.com/bigtravel-paperback

CHAPTER 5

BE THE LANDLORD

Deer in the Headlights

"Yes, I have chuzo de pollo, *hot dogs, hamburgers, and . . ."*

"Okay, give me a chuzo de pollo, *please," I repeated for the second time in Spanish.*

"Yes, there is chuzo de pollo *. . ." the street vendor said again.*

"Yeah, give me the chuzo de pollo!" *I spat out with frustration for the third time.*

A vacant stare came across the man's face as if I were an alien from another planet, speaking a totally different language than his native tongue. After months in Colombia, my Spanish was pretty good and I never had problems ordering food.

I looked over at Andrea thoroughly confused and quite frustrated that I was seemingly unable to order a simple thing that I'd done dozens of times before. She finally said to the man, "He wants

61

chuzo de pollo," *and he responded,* "*Ah, okay,* a la orden!*"*

He immediately began cooking the delicious chicken on a stick as we sat on a nearby bench taking a break from salsa dancing in the hot and humid El Tibiri *bar in Medellin.*

We both burst out in laughter as we sat down about just how difficult that experience was for me while Andrea assured me that I was indeed speaking very clearly.

The man, unaccustomed to gringos speaking fluent Spanish, basically became a "deer in the headlights" and could literally not comprehend what I was saying, no matter how many times I repeated it.

The Sharing Economy

Today's new sharing economy opens up a whole new world of possibilities where owners can rent out something they are not using—from cars and bicycles to spare bedrooms. These are but a few of the most popular scenarios in the sharing economy.

Airbnb is a peer-to-peer lodging service, which allows you to either rent out extra space in your home or apartment and allows travelers to find and book rooms that appeal to them because the rooms are often (but not always) cheaper than a hotel and because they provide the convenience of a home (kitchen, living room, etc) with more of a local flair.

Game Changer

For me, Airbnb has been an absolute game changer.

I had used Airbnb as a traveler a few times and enjoyed the experience. I feel like you get a better value through most Airbnb rentals for the reasons mentioned above than other forms of lodging, like traditional hotels.

There are a number of ways that you can use Airbnb to save money in order to travel or reduce your costs while traveling:

- Rent out space in your current place of residence to reduce your overhead and save more money for your upcoming travels.
- Use Airbnb as you travel to find cheaper lodging in

more off-the-beaten-path areas (not the higher priced tourist hot spots or hotels).

- Rent an apartment in the area you want to travel to and rent out the extra rooms to fellow travelers in order to cover your costs while overseas.

Reducing your overall costs per month can be huge for people struggling to pay off debt, those looking to pocket extra cash for big upcoming plans or purchases, or, as I suggest here, a viable option for people who would like to live overseas and need to keep costs extremely low during the process.

That last option, renting an apartment overseas in a place you want to live for a while, is exactly what I did in Medellin, Colombia. I didn't plan on doing it when I arrived in Colombia. I didn't even plan on staying in the city, but I just sort of fell for Medellin and decided I wanted to stick around for a little longer, work on my Spanish, and get to know the place better.

That's the beauty of spontaneous long-term travel—things you never even considered can end up happening.

That's also where I ended up meeting Andrea, so that might have had something to do with it as well . . .

To make my stay more affordable, I rented a three-bedroom apartment and rented out the two extra rooms via Airbnb to foreign backpackers (mostly fellow gringo Americans, Europeans, and Australians passing through) for a few nights or sometimes up to a week.

In my first full month using the service, I was able to cover 100% of the cost of my rent and utilities by hosting visitors, all with only a 35% occupancy rate over the month. So, yes, it's also possible to turn a profit with Airbnb.

Indeed, you can read story after story of those who, while sometimes going to extreme measures, were able to make $25,000 in a year or more in profit by renting their homes and extra space on Airbnb.

However, that isn't the goal here. We're just looking to

try and dramatically reduce expenses.

The initial steps are the same, though people working with their existing homes will be limited to what they have while those searching for something new with the intent of renting on Airbnb will have more flexibility to find a space that suits their needs.

I was paying $425 per month for a large three-bedroom apartment in a desirable neighborhood and charging $20 per night on average for each of the two extra rooms, meaning I only needed occupants for less than half the month (22 nights between both rooms, or about 11 nights in each room) to fully cover my rent.

Short-term furnished rooms obviously command higher prices than you would get if you were to have a fulltime roommate with whom you split the costs equally. Therefore, you can charge more, cover more of your costs, and maybe even make money.

During my best months, I fully covered my rent and utilities thanks to my Airbnb guests. During the slowest months, I was still able to reduce my total expenses by a hundred dollars or more.

Just to elaborate on the math, even if I were to pay $15 per night in a hostel dorm room (the going rate in Colombia), I would have been looking at $450 per month, which was around what I was paying for my large three-bedroom apartment with no guests. Indeed, having just one guest in a month meant it would be cheaper for me than a hostel and would allow me to have my own space, with my own bed and own kitchen, all while exploring a new and totally foreign place for the ensuing months.

Airbnb Landlord Model

The Airbnb Landlord Model (ALM) is one of the most exciting approaches for those who wish to travel and live overseas while really immersing themselves in a place, whether it is for the language, culture, food, or whatever may bring them abroad.

I have friends back home in Seattle that are paying as

much for a studio apartment as I was paying for my total cost of living for a month with a three-bedroom apartment, utilities, food, traveling, and so forth, and that's *before* any income from Airbnb guests.

With the Airbnb Landlord Model, I was able to reduce my total cost of living during the busiest months to just about $600–700 per month since I was effectively living rent-free. How is that for cheap?

Living Large

Just to be clear, I wasn't living in a hovel. Far from it. I had a nice place, in a good neighborhood, with fast Internet. I'd go out to eat regularly for tasty local food that only cost about $4 (soup/appetizer, full entree, and fresh fruit juice), and go for beers at the neighborhood bar for $1 each. That $600 per month also covered weekend trips outside of town, date nights with Andrea, and so forth. Six hundred dollars per month may sound ridiculously cheap to those used to the high prices of Europe or the States and may lead them to believe I'm living in squalor in the Third World.

Some people may say, "I'm not going to go to some backward, third world country just to save a few bucks!"— which is completely crazy—because I was readily enjoying a higher standard of living in Medellin, Colombia than I was when living in Washington DC, where I was making a steady income and living blocks from the US Capitol Building.

Medellin, despite it's turbulent past, is a modern, desirable city with a bustling nightlife and friendly locals. It even offers things that handily beat its US counterparts . . . I'm not really into malls, but they've got opulent malls with retractable roofs and even touchscreen monitors, in which you can punch your license plate to show you the exact location of your car in the massive parking garages. We are talking high tech.

The real kicker is that the only time I've ever been robbed in my life was, guess where . . . A few blocks from my place in Washington, DC, walking home one night.

The power of the ALM is not that you're going to poor, unsafe, or undesirable parts of the world, but rather the fact that you're leveraging the reality of geoarbitrage—using your dollars in a country where your money goes much, much further, thus allowing you to dramatically increase your standard of living. I was earning money in dollars via my Airbnb guests and paying my rent in pesos.

Enough about Medellin though; this is a model that can be viable in most parts of the world, so long as there is a moderate amount of tourist traffic passing through. Indeed, with the hotel industry revolting and many cities in the US instituting laws to curb the sharing economy, it can be much easier to launch the Airbnb Landlord Model abroad than at home.

If you're launching the Airbnb Landlord Model domestically, your rent will obviously be much higher, but you can also command higher prices per night as well. If you're trying to launch locally, be sure to research any laws or regulations that might impact your new rental property.

If you're serious about traveling overseas and traveling on the cheap, I would highly recommend taking a closer look at this Airbnb Landlord Model to see if it is a viable approach. Be sure to check out the site NomadList.io that can provide a great starting point to research the cost of living if you're considering doing this overseas.

If you're new to Airbnb, you can receive a free $25 credit toward your first stay as a guest. It's a great deal—enough for a free night in many overseas destinations.

Bottom Line

In order to take this approach overseas, there is a high barrier to entry that requires you to secure an apartment and possibly furnish it before you can get started with your Airbnb listing. This approach is suited to longer-term stays (the longer the better) and also requires a bit of research to ensure it is viable. If you are taking this approach to reduce costs at your current place of residence, there is a minimal barrier to entry, just creating your listing.

After getting started, it is fairly low effort to maintain— just responding to emails from potential guests, coordinating arrival times, and cleaning up between visitors.

Taking this approach allowed me to save as much as 100% of my rent and utilities, more than $450 per month, and even slow months resulted in savings compared to what I would have paid in a hostel dorm, albeit with much better accommodations. Savings and income will vary based on geographic area, tourist demand, and other factors.

In order to stay within your $1,200 budget for a month, you would want to cover close to 100% of your rent and utilities (regardless of where you are in the world), leaving you with $40 per day for food and activities, an amount that you can easily work with. In this case, I was able to live on around $600 per month ($20 per day for food and activities) during my busiest months. You could use your savings from Airbnb guests to live more extravagantly by increasing your daily expenses.

How to Get Started

The first step is to get on Airbnb and research other rentals in your current locale or desired future residence.

Browse through nearby listings to get an idea of the going nightly rate and take a look at the number of reviews the top properties have received.

In my experience, the number of actual stays and guests is significantly higher than the amount of people who leave reviews for a listing—just like my book on Amazon.com, don't forget to leave a review when you finish!

Higher rates per night and a number of properties with a significant amount of reviews is a great sign that there is both demand in the area and room for additional hosts.

Run the numbers based on the cash flow that you would need: How many nights would you need to rent to reach the extra income desired? How much would you need to pay your rent or mortgage completely? If you had a slow month with 10% occupancy, do the numbers still make sense?

If your rent is $800 per month and you could charge $50 per night, you are looking at 16 nights per month, which is a 50% occupancy rate. A 50% occupancy rate or below is a good target—you will neither achieve a 100% percent occupancy, nor do you probably want a 100% occupancy, which would entail same-day turnover between guests when you may like to have a day or two between new arrivals.

If you have a significant gap in your pricing to occupancy ratio (i.e., you would need 90% occupancy to fully cover your costs), then you may not be able to earn as much as you would like in order to live rent-free, but it can still help reduce overall costs.

If you are settling in a new area with the goal of renting on Airbnb to cover your costs, as I did, it may very well be better to rent a larger than needed place with more than one room that you can rent simultaneously.

My rent was $425 per month, and I had two rooms available for rent in my three-bedroom apartment—a small room with a twin bed and shared bath, and a larger room with a double bed and private bath.

I charged different prices for each room for an average price of $20 per night. That means I needed approximately 22 nights of occupancy in total between the two rooms for a roughly 35% occupancy rate.

In reality I got a lot of couples that came for the larger room with a private bath, and you can add a nominal extra charge for a second person (I charged $5 more), which in practice means that I could successfully hit $425 per month with a 50% occupancy of couples in that room alone.

About Tourist Season

Take into account the local tourism season and weather. Do people come for the snow or for the sun? Or only during summer for the great weather and access to the beach? Or is there a more stable supply of year-round visitation?

If you believe that this model is viable for your geographic area, the next step may be to furnish the property or extra room.

I want to speak about this as a model for world travel and taking up temporary residence somewhere abroad because while costs will vary tremendously around the world, the basic idea is the same.

To Furnish ... Or Not

If you are starting from scratch, renting an unfurnished apartment with the goal of renting it out, you need to take into consideration the cost of furnishing the apartment and how long you will be staying.

The unfurnished apartment model doesn't work easily for short stays, but if you are looking at staying somewhere for at least six months, I believe that it really starts to make sense.

For instance, I had to spend a little more than $700 out of pocket (and up front) to furnish my three-bedroom apartment in Medellin.

When you consider that I was staying there for about 6 months, the cost per month to furnish it amounts to a little over $100. You are also able to make up some of that money by selling it off at the end of your stay.

It is best to furnish your apartment with second-hand items whenever possible, so as to not lose so much to depreciation. You really only need the bare essentials to go forward renting it out—bed, nightstand, and space for clothes in the bedroom, along with a furnished kitchen (at least the basics) and some furnishing in the common areas like a sofa and chair, desk, table, etc. I would skip big-ticket items like television and cable since most guests are there to explore a place, not to watch TV. WiFi and Internet are essential, obviously.

Local Rules and Regs

You should also be aware of any local rules or regulations either in the city or country you choose, as well as on a property by property basis—some apartments will not permit you to rent out rooms or may not permit subleasing. In many cases, it is easier to rent a house where you are offered more leeway.

And the Extras

There will be a few extra costs related to running your Airbnb Empire. You will need to buy a few sets of extra sheets and towels to swap between guests. You will go through extra toilet paper, soap, and use more water and electricity, which will raise your utility bills. You may want to consider bringing on a weekly cleaning service to help out, which I did and was absolutely worth it, both for me personally and for the Airbnb guests.

These are all things to keep in mind while pricing and running the numbers.

Your Profile

The next step is to create your Airbnb profile if you are just getting started. Fill in lots of information in your profile and about yourself, verify your identity with your official government IDs, and link your profile to as many social media platforms as you have.

This step is important. Guests want to know they can trust this stranger they are going to stay with and want to know a little bit about them.

While people using Airbnb aren't expecting (or wanting) a hotel experience, they want to get a sense that you are normal, respectful, easy going, etc. This isn't couchsurfing; they are still paying for a place to stay and want to feel comfortable and at home while they are there.

Another important step when you are beginning is to get as many references from friends and family as possible. Under the profile options, you can request references from people you know (you have to submit an official request to an individual on the website before they are able to leave you a reference). Don't neglect this step.

List your property and space. Be thorough—there is no such thing as too much information or too many photos for this section.

Take nice photos for your property, or bring in one of Airbnb's professional photographers to shoot your property (a free service, but not available in all areas, which also shows that your listing is accurate and not just photos of some luxurious villa you downloaded from the Internet).

Craft a compelling title and description. I won't get into sales psychology here, but you should be trying to convince guests that they want to stay at your property. "Cozy room" is definitely an improvement over "cramped, claustrophobic room."

That being said, don't lie about your listing or set false expectations for guests, or you are inviting negative reviews down the road.

Talk openly and honestly about the good aspects of your property while mentioning directly some of the potential downsides (no view, moderate street noise, etc). What works and appeals to one person might not appeal to another. Some people want to be in the heart of the action where the nightlife is while others prefer a quiet countryside retreat.

Landing the Initial Review

How do you get your first reviews? This is the hardest part when starting out. With no reviews, no one wants to stay there, and since Airbnb sorts by popularity, almost no one sees your listing. If no one sees it, no one will stay there, and you'll never get your first review. Catch-22.

I just suggest that you ask a friend or family member (who has actually been to your place) to officially book a night through your Airbnb listing. You can lower the price just for them, invite them over, play host, and get your first review.

Some may consider this slightly unethical, and padding your reviews definitely isn't cool. I only suggest this as an option to jump-start your listing and getting that oh-so-difficult first review. After that, be sure to just run things as normal. But once you have that initial review, you'll probably begin getting inquiries.

Airbnb search results are sorted for potential guests primarily based on popularity and the number of reviews a property has received while also taking into account the host's account activity and responsiveness to inquiries.

Therefore, be sure to respond to guests as soon as possible and to update your calendar frequently (even if only to mark the current evening as "not available").

Temporary Discount

When you first launch your listing, the best strategy you can take is to list below your desired rate and below market rate in order to attract your next few visitors and more reviews. You can even directly mention that your rates are discounted temporarily for this reason in your listing.

As you get started, it is preferable to have lots of short-term stays rather than longer visitors, that is to say that five guests for a night or two is better than one guest for a week, in the beginning. This brings in more potential reviews (always nicely remind guests to leave a review when you say goodbye) and better rankings in Airbnb because they consider quantity of reviews, not how long a guest may have stayed.

The downside is more initial work created due to guest turnover with cleaning, changing sheets, and preparing rooms.

Over time you can (and should) raise your rates and be more selective with your guests. Later on, it is preferable to take on longer-term visitors that will stay for a week or so versus short-term stays that cause more work between guests.

That's about it. Sit back and enjoy your new part-time

job in the hospitality industry!

By following the steps outlined above, you should be able to bring in some cash with your extra space, reduce your monthly costs, and maybe even live rent-free—all for very little work overall—just answering emails, greeting guests, and helping ensure they have a pleasant stay while providing recommendations for things to see and do in the area.

And Don't Worry

Some people worry about inviting strangers into their homes. They worry about thefts, people breaking things, or inviting weirdos into their house.

First, with Airbnb you can reject anyone you want without giving a real reason. You don't like the way they come across from their emails, you don't like the photo of them partying, no references, whatever. If for any reason you get a bad vibe from someone in the initial communication, just say no.

Second, Airbnb does have a generous insurance policy that will cover you in the event of theft or damages—but nothing like that ever happened to me.

I will say that not every guest and experience will be 100% ideal, but that overall I found the experience to be quite pleasant, fun, and I even made long-term connections with a few guests.

I haven't had a bad experience with anyone per se, but there have been some guests that annoyed me more than others . . .

People that would hoard dishes inside their room for the whole stay (when I didn't have a huge amount of plates and cups), play their music without headphones, or one guy who used the nice hand soap in the bathroom as his personal body wash.

As for actual problems, I've had a few simple occurrences, like people locking themselves out of their rooms, arrival delays due to the airlines, dishes being accidentally broken, but never anything major.

All in all, it was a really pleasant experience—hopefully for both parties.

It was also somewhat fun to play tour guide for my newly adopted city by providing my favorite recommendations for things to see and do in town, including some that were off the beaten tourist trail and that allowed my guests to see something they wouldn't have otherwise seen.

Whether you would like to reduce your living costs back home in the States in order to pay down your debt faster and save money for a future trip, or want to jet off to some far-flung corner of the world and live on the cheap while you launch your Next Big Thing, I think Airbnb provides an amazing opportunity to all.

Q and A

How long does it take to find a place and furnish it?

Finding a place that meets your criteria quickly can be a challenge, especially overseas. You will be best served by trying to do as much legwork as possible before arrival—researching neighborhoods, costs, hurdles, real estate agents that can show you around. Many cities around the world have expat- or foreigner-focused Facebook groups, which can help you make many of those crucial connections and references. Keep an eye out for expats that may be leaving the country permanently and allow you to either take over their leases or their belongings.

If you can't do much research in advance, you can book a few nights on Airbnb with a foreign/expat host (not a local) and talk to them openly about your plans. They've already gone through the process and are probably more than happy to help you navigate the waters and point you in the right direction if you are considering a long-term stay.

I was in Medellin for a month or two before making the decision that I wanted to stay for the rest of the year, and I lucked out finding another gringo who would soon be leaving. I was thus able to assume the rent of their apartment and buy the furnishings directly off of them. If you are starting from scratch, you can probably expect the process to take a month or two to be able to rent it out, unless you have particularly good connections or an existing familiarity with a place.

How long can you stay overseas?

This varies from country to country depending on the visa you will be receiving. Six months is a common number for many places across the world, which provides you with a good chunk of time to explore a place and is sufficient to launch the Airbnb Landlord Model if you hit the ground running.

Sometimes you can make a "visa run" to neighboring countries (or pay a professional or an agency to make the run for you) in order to extend your time as well.

Research options for student visas, which often don't require much more than enrolling in a local university for language classes and permit you to stay in most countries longer than a normal tourist visa.

Be sure to visit the State Department website or the equivalent in your respective country to identify the possible length of stay and any bureaucratic complications that travelers should be aware of as they arrive or leave.

Anna's Story

Anna Filipski connected with me initially via my blog and later asked to read a preview copy of this book. As a fellow nomad, she actually has experience using each of tactics mentioned in this book successfully, including the Airbnb Landlord Model. Here's Anna's story:

I rented a place in Tempe, Arizona because I knew I would be there at least 6 months. I grew up in Tempe and have family and friends there but hadn't been there in a while so wanted to spend a little more time than a short vacation there. Most friends now have families, and I am too old for full-time roommates any more, and I wasn't about to live with family. I had friends that did Airbnb near downtown Phoenix successfully, so I decided that a place near the university would probably do well. I did a little research before making this decision.

I found a cute place near the university with 3 bedrooms and a yard for my dog—something I could certainly not afford on my own but I decided to take a risk. The rent was $1,200 per month.

I found a friend who wanted to rent one room for her office as a midwife. She was only there during the day 2–3 days a week and paid me $350 per month.

The other room was for Airbnb guests. I paid about $400 for a mattress and furniture for the room. I bought maybe $200 more worth of furniture for myself for the rest of the house. I actually set up the account before I even moved in and was booked from 2 days after I moved in! I had to get things together quickly. My ad on Airbnb mentions that I am a minimalist and have very little. People actually seemed to love that about it. Very little clutter and an awesome dog.

My average monthly income with Airbnb was $600 (roughly 40% occupancy rate). So, I only ended up paying about $250 a month plus utilities. I was charging $50 per night for 4 out of 5 months. When it started getting hot around the summer, things started to slow down, so I dropped my rate to $35 just to fill as much as I could until I moved out.

My landlord didn't know what I was doing, but I was confident that they wouldn't mind. It is certainly a risk and a good idea to feel things out in your community of choice where you will be renting to ensure that it is not a breach to their contract.

I even made a few really good friends among the guests that stayed with me. I only had one bad experience (it wasn't scary bad, just annoying) where a couple came home from a bachelorette party at 3 a.m. and had a very loud fight for about 30 minutes! So dumb. But in 5 months, if that was the worst of it, I'd say that's pretty great.

When it came time to move on, I sold most of the furniture via Craigslist and to friends on Facebook and gave a bit away as well.

I would definitely do it again in the future. I actually loved it and met so many wonderful people without the problems of having the same person there all the time and definitely made more money doing it than I would have with a roommate. It was a dream.

I enjoy the nomadic lifestyle and what I do, and I choose to live a minimalist lifestyle. People always ask how I do it, but I have no answers. I just follow my heart and everything seems to work out.

Big Chapter, Small Summary

• Today's sharing economy offers an exciting new model for overseas travel.

• Eliminate one of your biggest expenses: lodging.

• Get the temporary expat experience and free up your time for really getting to know a place, learning the language, or launching a freelance side hustle.

Benefits

• *Expat + Backpacker Experience*
One of the best reasons to stay in a hostel is to meet fellow travelers, but then you're stuck in some terrible dorm room with eight other people. This approach allows the home renter to get a little bit of that social experience abroad by inviting in traveling guests and occasionally heading out with them for a meal or drink. I like meeting fellow travelers and really enjoyed opening up my temporary home to them. But it's also got the advantage of my being able to reject the stays of potential guests if I wanted my own space and no guests on the weekend, for

example.

- *Geoarbitrage—if you head overseas*

This is one of the biggest advantages of heading to certain overseas destinations—your dollars go much, much further for almost everything. Guests pay in dollars, and you pay your rent in local currency. Big meals at local restaurants for $4 instead of $14 at home. I got a dental crown done for $250 instead of $1,000+. My total cost of living in a month was what some friends pay for their studio apartments back home.

- *Home Base for Entrepreneurial Activities*

Many people would love to break into freelancing or build a location-independent business online, but the cost of living domestically can be so high that they can't afford to leave their jobs and dedicate themselves to getting started. The Airbnb Landlord Model allows you to leverage geoarbitrage overseas to live cheaply as you really focus on getting things off the ground.

Drawbacks

- *Too Much Stuff*

One of the reasons I love travel is the simplicity of it and how it forces you to evaluate what is truly important, especially as it relates to what you pack and bring along. After the freedom of a year of overlanding, which itself is an exercise in forced minimalism, I was forced to downsize further still as I traveled by backpack, and then, all of a sudden I had an apartment full of furniture and things. It was a little overwhelming!

- *Bureaucratic Complications*

This is one that depends on the part of the world in which you plan to employ this tactic, but you have to consider the time allowed on your visa, if there are significant barriers to rent an apartment, particularly related to utilities, obtaining Internet, and whether or not you're allowed to sublease as such with Airbnb. This approach is the most logistically complicated tactic in this book and may not be for everyone, but it is a very powerful method that deserves consideration.

Resources and Further Reading

- Website: Airbnb – airbnb.com

Sign up with the largest and most well-known temporary rental site. If you're new to the world of Airbnb, you can get started with my link (www.desktodirtbag.com/airbnb) and claim a $25 credit absolutely free, which you can apply toward your first stay as a guest.

- Blog Post: My Airbnb Listing in Medellin

Check out a PDF copy of my actual Airbnb listing in Colombia, photos of my place, along with a handy calculator that can help you calculate the occupancy rate you would need in order to cover your rent.

- Book: *Get Paid for Your Pad*

If you're looking for more detailed resources about how to be most successful with your new Airbnb empire, I can think of no better resource than the *Get Paid for Your Pad* ebook and video course.

- Book: *Airbnb Pro*

"Airbnb Pro" from Making It Anywhere is another excellent resource that I used on the path to success with my apartment in Medellin. It has all sorts of nuggets of wisdom that go far beyond what I explained here.

For links to all the resources and materials mentioned in this chapter, be sure to visit:

www.desktodirtbag.com/bigtravel-paperback

CHAPTER 6

PLAY WITH PETS

No Bull

We just fed the horses their morning hay and were walking back to the house when we noticed a trail of hoof prints all around the outside of the horse corral. "What the . . . ?"

We were looking after a ranch house in the mountains of Baja California, Mexico and the property was fenced off, so no other big animals should be able to enter. Andrea and I followed the prints around the property until they petered out in the grass. There was no sign that an animal was still around, so we went about our day.

Later that evening I opened the door to feed the animals again, and that's when he decided to show himself . . . a big white bull stared at me from about 15 feet away, I'd interrupted him as he was munching on the home's landscaping.

The two cattle dogs, Wags and Pepita, sat in their doghouses nearby and looked on with disinterest.

Herding cows is not exactly my specialty—and I'm definitely not big on intimidating bulls. I've seen videos of what those things can do during the running of the bulls in Spain.

Wielding a shovel, I slowly made my way over to the big bull, calling for Wags and Pepita to back me up, as I shouted at him and shooed him away from the house.

Andrea slipped around and opened the main gate to the driveway, and the dogs and I managed to send him packing after a lot of effort and a few wrong turns.

We thought we were rid of our problem, but he managed to return again the next day, as the delicious greenery inside the finca *was just too good to resist.*

Beloved Animals

So, you read the previous chapter about launching your Airbnb Empire, and now I hear you saying, "But Ryan, I don't want to be tied down with an apartment rental on Airbnb—I want to be free to travel!"

I hear you. If you're looking for the freedom to travel virtually anywhere while not paying any money for lodging, then you're definitely going to want to take a look at the world of house and pet sitting.

For those of you unfamiliar with the concept, house sitting is where an owner seeks out someone to come in for a period of time to stay at their place and (almost always) take care of their beloved animals while they are traveling or away.

The homeowner gets the peace of mind of having someone around to look after their home and make sure everything is okay while also allowing their pet to stay in the familiarity of home while being able to save hundreds of dollars that they would otherwise spend to board their pet in a temporary shelter. The house sitter (you) gets to stay at a place rent-free, with a new area to explore, and even a temporary pet to play with (a definite plus if you love animals but can't easily have one due to your newfound nomadic lifestyle).

House sitting gigs can be especially appealing as you

continue to travel for longer periods of time and begin to find yourself occasionally longing for the privacy and amenities that having your own place offers. Sometimes the call of domesticity can be pretty strong after you've been on the road—and house sitting can be a great way to break up your travels. It's really a pretty awesome exchange that benefits both parties.

House sitting opportunities are extremely varied with offerings from the heart of Manhattan to small coastal villages in Costa Rica. There are palatial estates with pools or humble homes in the center of town. Some are easy work, simply caring for a sleepy cat, while others may be more demanding if you must care for a handful of dogs (or even farm animals). Some are for a long weekend while others are for half a year or longer.

As I write this, I am strung up in a hammock at a house sit in the mountains of Baja California in Mexico. We are at an extremely remote, off the grid, solar-powered home on more than 1,000 acres, as we look after two ranch dogs, two retired horses, and a few chickens. This is our home for the month and has provided an excellent break during our long-term overlanding trip for us to recharge a bit and live ridiculously cheap. We're way out in the country (two hours one-way to the supermarket), so there isn't really any way to spend money besides on our groceries.

Our day-to-day schedule is decidedly normal: Get up and feed the animals, make breakfast for ourselves, get some work done (like writing this book), have lunch, take a siesta, maybe work some more or take care of household chores, go for a walk or trail run in the late afternoon, feed the animals again, watch the sunset over the hills, and maybe cap off the night with some TV or a movie.

It is hard to paint an all-encompassing picture of house sitting duties when they can be so widely varied, but regardless, I'm sure you can find something that meets your desired level of commitment, work, and location.

House sitting can be nice to break up longer journeys

where you are frequently camping, in hostels or hotels, or just generally on the move. I ended up renting that apartment in Medellin for the Airbnb Landlord Model because, after a year and a half of constantly being on the go, I just kind of felt the call to settle down even for just a little bit.

House sitting can allow you to relax, live like a local, download your photos to send to family, cook in a real kitchen, and otherwise just catch up on things, even if it's just for a week or two.

I love house sitting, and we are constantly on the look out for new opportunities down the road to live rent-free.

If you have flexibility with your time and location as you would likely have on a long-term trip, a whole new world of opportunities opens up to you with a whole slew of possible travel experiences. There are listings all over the world from France, the UK, Australia, all over the States, Central America, and beyond.

Dale and Franca have been hopping around Europe and living like locals while taking care of people's pets and enjoying all that Europe has to offer but doing it much more affordably.

Dalene and Pete Heck have saved more than $30,000 in accommodation costs through house sitting over the years.

House sitting is definitely growing in popularity, but it is still a relatively underground phenomenon that few people take advantage of.

Are you ready to give house sitting a try?

Bottom Line

In order to take this approach, there is a moderate barrier to entry, which requires that you join a membership site, fill out your profile, apply for listings, be interviewed, and then be accepted by the homeowner.

After getting started, there is a range of effort required based on particular house sits, but it is pretty low effort to feed and look after 1–2 dogs or cats (the most typical assignments).

Taking this approach allowed me to save at least $50–100 per night compared to a hotel room—two weeks would be $700 to $1,400 or more—much, much more money if I were to stay in a hotel for a month or if I considered renting an equivalent size home on Airbnb or VRBO.com.

In order to stay within your $1,200 budget, you would be limited to $40 per day for food and activities, since you are not paying for accommodations. Free lodging allows you to spend a greater amount of money per day while staying under budget, and having access to a full kitchen allows you to cook one or two meals per day and save money. House sitting is especially well suited to expensive cities that may not otherwise be affordable to those on a budget. But you can also find more rural retreats and spend dramatically less money per month.

How to Get Started
Choose a Site

The first step is to register with a house sitting service. There are many, many different websites out there, but the one that we use is Trusted House Sitters.

Most house sitting websites are membership based (i.e., they do cost a little bit of money to get started) to ensure that everyone is active in the community. The fee basically pays for itself as soon as you land that first house sitting gig. The websites are the easiest way to get started and seek out a variety of opportunities across a large geographic area, though some people also find success purely through word of mouth.

I use and fully recommend TrustedHouseSitters.com, which is one of the largest and most geographical diverse house sitting sites on the Internet. I'd recommend starting there unless you have a specific geographic advantage with another website.

The fee for Trusted House Sitters depends on how long you sign up, but if you land just one house sitting gig during that time, the membership will have paid for itself.

A three-month plan with them goes for $23.99 per month—or you can get the annual plan for just $7.99 per month (a single payment of $95.88).

You can also sign up through my link (www.desktodirtbag.com/housesitters) and get a 20% discount on the prices above.

Your Profile

Once you've registered with your chosen house sitting website, the next key step is to set up a killer profile. Don't neglect this step. Some house sitting listings will receive dozens of inquiries from eager house sitters competing for a prime location or a particularly swanky place.

Think about selling points from the homeowners' perspective—they are first and foremost concerned about finding reliable, responsible, trustworthy people who are going to look after their home and their furry little loved ones.

Select a number of photos that demonstrate your love of animals and your maturity. Non-staged photos with different animals go over the best. Now is not the time to use those photos from spring break . . .

Video Intro

On most sites you also have the option of creating a video introduction. A simple two-minute video introducing yourself, why you want to house sit, your experience with animals, and so forth can really help home owners get a sense of the person they might be having in their home.

The most important thing is to emphasize that you are a responsible person who will take good care of their pets and home—and hopefully that really is you, and you aren't going to lie about it.

External References

As you start your profile, you can and should build up your references from outside sources as well. Perhaps you've house sat for friends or watched their pets for a bit? Ask them to write you an external reference. You can also request references from landlords, employers, or other friends and family. External references don't carry as much weight, but they are important to have in the beginning as you try to land your first gig.

Background Check, Maybe

As an extra boost of confidence, you can also request a police check that will appear on your profile, giving homeowners the peace of mind that you aren't a convicted criminal. That's not something I've done as of yet, and we haven't had a problem landing assignments.

Going, Going—Gone!

New listings can come online and then stop accepting applications unexpectedly fast as a homeowner gets flooded with applications, particularly if the listing is in a popular travel destination or is an especially appealing home.

To best increase your odds, you should be watching the site diligently. With Trusted House Sitters you can get email notifications of new listings within the geographic areas you designate.

Try your best to stay on top of the new listings, and apply early in order to be at the top of their list.

Pro Tip: For particularly competitive house sits, you can upload a quick, private YouTube video for each house sit you apply for and send them the link in your initial email. This will make your application stand out among the rest and will give your application a much more personal touch.

Be Selective

Don't just copy and paste and apply for everything you possibly can. Be selective and be sure to tailor your emails to each individual home by using their names and the names of their pets, whenever possible.

Closer to Home

If you are not yet traveling but are hoping to line up house sitting gigs in the future as you are embarking on a longer-term trip, I would certainly encourage you to look at house sitting gigs closer to home. This will allow you to build up your first real references and get a better sense of what house sitting entails.

Face-to-Face

If you leave a good first impression with your initial email, the next step will most likely be a request for a telephone or Skype interview to chat "face-to-face" and give each party a chance to better to get to know one another.

While you may be excited at the prospect of landing your first possible house sit, please bear in mind that they are not just interviewing you for the job, but you should also be interviewing them to ensure it is a good fit.

Ask lots of questions:

- Ask about what the pet's/s' needs are in terms of food, care, medicine, exercise; whether they are prone to having accidents, etc.

- Ask about how long you can be away from the animals and house during the day.

- Ask about additional responsibilities they might have for you around the house, from watering plants to checking the mail.

- Ask about the location, whether you'll need a car, and how far you would be from groceries, other necessities, and any attractions you would like to see.

- Ask about how much communication they expect or would like while they are away (some like to hear from you regularly, others less frequently).

Yes, ask lots of questions; it isn't bad. Indeed, it will show that you know what you are talking about, are experienced, and aren't just willing to take whatever house sit you can find.

That's the gist of it. If all goes well, you will both be on board for the house sit. Be sure to stay in contact as the date approaches to make sure that everything is still good to go. This is especially important if you will be traveling long distance for a house sit.

Commonly—and Less Commonly

The most common approach to house sitting is by planning a house sit based around where you would like to travel or to find opportunities that present themselves along your ongoing travels. But I have heard of more unconventional approaches where people have gotten rid of their apartments and bounce from house sitting gig to house sitting gig within their own city where they normally work and live.

By doing this, they can save hundreds upon hundreds of dollars that they would otherwise be using to pay for rent and utilities, and they can better use that money toward paying down their debts or sticking it in their travel funds.

It's kind of like they are nomads in their own hometowns. I like it. Couple that with a solid overlanding rig to use between gigs, and you've got an extremely low overhead lifestyle that will enable you to escape debt and save money.

Another approach for those with the conventional trappings of an apartment would be to seek out house sitting opportunities within their local area—as mentioned above—but then once you land a house sitting gig, you could advertise those days as available on Airbnb while you are away and pocket the money. You can command much higher prices by renting out a full house instead of a single bedroom.

This approach would allow you to build up your references and profile on both services, which will do wonders in the long run as you pursue other house sits or Airbnb guests.

Like Airbnb, references can make or break you. It will make it much harder to land that dream house sitting gig down the road if you've got a big fat zero next to the references section on your profile. If you've got the time, I would highly recommend to start house sitting by seeking out local opportunities.

My Start

Andrea and I got started in exactly that way. We put together a decent profile to start with and began applying for local opportunities. We found a two-week house sit located about an hour away from my hometown (where we had been staying on and off between smaller road trips in Washington State).

Since we decided to start locally, we didn't do the Skype interview but instead traded a few emails, had a quick phone call, and then just headed out to the potential house sit to meet the owners and their dog, Daisy, see the house, and go over all the details.

I think an in-person interview is best for all parties involved, whenever possible. It will give you a full and accurate idea of what you will be doing, what the pet is like, where you'll be staying, and so forth. And particularly if you have limited references, you will be able to make a better impression on the homeowners.

In exchange for a beautiful home to live in with all the comforts one could ask for, we just had to take care of Daisy, their sweet, lovable dachshund. We were able to live in a beautiful two-bedroom, two-bath home just outside of Seattle with blazing fast WiFi, full on cable with premium channels and DVR, a large, fenced-in backyard, and a lovely modern kitchen with all the amenities. And best of all, we weren't paying anything for it.

During those two weeks, it only cost us about $80–100 for food for both of us. We had no expenses for cable, Internet, heating, or rent.

That is truly dirt-cheap living.

Daisy was absolutely easygoing, and we loved being around her. We felt at ease and at home during our first ever house sit, and it was even a little hard saying goodbye to Daisy when they returned!

House sitting is pretty awesome, I gotta say. Indeed, if you're at all considering or hoping to undertake long-term travel, then you should definitely be looking at house sitting. It is one of the big "secrets" of those of us who continue to travel year after year.

Q and A

Do you have to join a paid membership site?

Absolutely not. Obviously word of mouth is the old fashioned way: house sitting for friends of friends or shirttail relatives. But without previous experience and being plugged into a network of people looking for sitters, it certainly poses a number of additional difficulties, especially if you hope to travel farther away from home.

There are other house sitting sites on the Internet with differing price plans—be sure to check the resource section at the end of this chapter. There are also a number of Facebook groups related to house and pet sitting where people will informally offer their services or post opportunities. Those are other good places to start.

The power of the paid membership sites is in building a public profile with references that speak directly about your experience as a house sitter that can connect strangers on opposite sides of the world.

I do not mind paying a modest fee for the convenience of the service and the breadth of opportunities available.

Is this available to me as a (insert demographic here)?

There are house sitters of all ages, colors, sexual identities, etc. Above all, homeowners just want someone who is responsible, trustworthy, and who loves pets. If you are those things, then you've got a really good shot.

There is a general bias towards couples by homeowners though, primarily due to the fact that they have a built-in back up if one of you had a family emergency or other crisis that forced you to leave during your duties. Couples (particularly if they are younger) are also seen as more responsible or mature compared to young single folks (particularly guys), and aren't going to be "out on the town" all the time.

That isn't to say that if you are single that house sitting isn't possible, indeed there are many young single people (both guys and girls) who have success with house sitting. But you will need to go the extra mile when competing against the applications of equally qualified couples. In this situation it is even more important to build up lots of character references and land your first assignments locally.

Do these house and pet sitting gigs offer anything beyond free compensation?

It isn't impossible to find opportunities that offer a small stipend for your services, but that isn't typically the norm. The compensation is primarily considered to be the free lodging and utilities paid by the homeowner in exchange for your care of their animals. Most homeowners will also offer up use of whatever is in the pantry and fridge. Certain assignments may provide a number of other amenities from hot tubs and pools to gyms and rooftops decks.

Some assignments don't even require the care of animals but are just looking for someone to stay in the house and ensure that all is well. The standard in that case, if it is a long-term house sit without pets, is that the sitter covers the cost of utilities during that period.

Another Ryan's Story

Ryan Biddulph is a fellow blogger and vagabond behind the Blogging from Paradise website. We connected virtually thanks to our similar perspectives on life and travel. Ryan and his wife Kelli have landed some pretty top-of-the-line house sitting gigs over the past year, so I asked Ryan if he'd be willing to share his perspective. Here's Ryan's story:

I've been house sitting for a little over a year with jobs in Fiji, Bali, and New York City. In each case I watched pets and kept an eye on the home. Much of the job was just being a live body inside of the house and making sure everything was okay around the property. At times I also ran errands like checking the mail, paying property taxes at the bank, and other simple tasks.

At our house sit in Jimbaran, Bali, we looked after an extensive property with four villas, three adorable little dogs, 35 chickens, a few cats, and lived in this tropical paradise with a stunning view of Jimbaran Bay that would otherwise command prices of hundreds or even thousands of dollars per night. And despite the 22-hour flight into the middle of nowhere in the Pacific Ocean, this house sit was an amazing opportunity to live for four months in Bali and really get to know the place like a local.

In my experience, it is extremely easy to find gigs, especially if you're open to house sitting in Europe, one of the most popular regions. My wife Kelli and I are picky though; we only house sit in the tropics (excluding New York City because it's only 30 minutes away from our home town), so we had to wait a little bit before we found those sits in Bali and Fiji. Those opportunities don't present themselves as frequently, and they are extremely competitive . . . I mean who wouldn't want to live on a tropical island paradise for a few months, absolutely rent free?

Europe, Australia, and the USA are all awesome spots of course, but we prefer Southeast Asia and the South Pacific. Since I own the site "Blogging from Paradise," I enjoy spending time in tropical locations, which align perfectly with my brand. Knowing this, we pick and choose our sits and never chase any sit that doesn't align with our preferences and ideal travel destinations. We are super transparent with the homeowner, sharing our blog and social media links, and we also chat with the homeowner on Skype to form bonds and quickly set ourselves apart from the other applicants.

I will pursue other ideal house sits in the future, but since we both earn a healthy income online and since our businesses are growing quickly, we may need to pull back a little bit, unless a particular sit really makes us sing. We've worked our tails off to be able to afford our travels while boosting our savings, which is in part thanks to house sitting.

Would I recommend house sitting to fellow long-term travelers? Oh yes! Do it . . . You'll absolutely love it.

Big Chapter, Small Summary

- Housesitting is one of the most accessible ways to dramatically reduce your lodging costs while traveling.

- For just a small investment in a membership website, you can be connected with hundreds of potential gigs from strangers all over the world.

- In exchange for a small time commitment taking care of other people's animals, you will open up a new world of affordable travel opportunities.

Benefits

- *Live absolutely rent- and utility-free.*

This allows you to save hundreds to thousands on accommodation costs.

- *Live like a local in an area off the beaten path where you aren't likely to encounter quite so many tourists.*

You'll also be able to live like a local by having a real house, not just a hotel room and a mini fridge, where you can save further money by cooking at home at least part of the time.

- *Take a break from the hustle and bustle of traditional travel.*

Those whirlwind trips are great . . . up to a point. Allow yourself to recharge with your own bed, a kitchen, and all the creature comforts that are often lacking while traveling.

- *Travel slow.*

You can see more and travel cheaper if you travel slowly. Sure, you could see gazillion countries in two months, or you could spend two months in the countryside of Tuscany and really immerse yourself in a place and the culture.

- *Get some work done.*

If you're a freelancer, it can be difficult to constantly work out of coffee shops and be on the hunt for WiFi. A house sit can provide a nice, reliable connection and quiet space to get some real work done.

- *Play with animals without the years of commitment that pet ownership entails.*

I love pets, but they definitely hinder a nomadic and spontaneous lifestyle. With house sitting, I can still get my fix with other people's adorable animals.

Drawbacks

- *Somewhat housebound.*

The level of commitment and work obviously varies from house sit to house sit, but you are committing to being there to feed and care for someone's animals. Usually this means you are free for the better part of the day but need to be around in the morning and early evening to feed them. Obviously this can impede other travel-related activities you might hope to do.

- *It is a job.*

Again, you need to be there as necessary to care for the animals, and you need to keep the place clean. The spontaneity of travel can take a hit because of the commitment factor. You will be tied to a particular place for a prearranged period of time, so if you're bored or itching to get on the move again, you won't be able to until the homeowners have returned.

Resources and Further Reading

- Website: Trusted House Sitters – trustedhousesitters.com

A one-year membership costs less than $99. You can receive a 20% discount on any plan through my link (www.desktodirtbag.com/housesitters).

- Website: House Carers – housecarers.com

Another large and popular house sitting website that you might want to consider joining along with Trusted House Sitters.

- Blog Post: My Behind the Scenes House Sitting

At my website, you can find more photos, stories, and details about some of our specific house sitting experiences.

- Course: House Sitting Academy

If you're looking for further resources to take your house sitting endeavors to the next level, the best out there is the House Sitting Academy by Nat and Jodie. They dive into all the nitty gritty aspects of becoming a successful house sitter, landing the most competitive gigs, and avoiding some of the most common pitfalls.

For links to all the resources and materials mentioned in this chapter, be sure to visit:

www.desktodirtbag.com/bigtravel-paperback

CHAPTER 7

WHY YOU WON'T TRAVEL

Don't Go Anywhere

"Where are you going?! You can't leave!"an old Colombian farmer shouted at us in Spanish.

My buddy Jeff and I were down at the local watering after a day of volunteering in the heat of the sun on a farm 45 minute outside of San Gil, Colombia. We were well off of the gringo trail, and this local bar certainly doesn't see too many foreigners.

After a few refreshing cervezas, *we were about to walk back to the farm for dinner with our volunteer host family.*

We got up to leave when the man stopped us, protesting our departure . . . Uh oh, what did we do?

The man was very difficult to understand, for both his strange and unfamiliar country accent and for my relatively novice command of the language at the time.

"You can't leave yet, it's still very early!"

"You sure you don't want another beer?"

"I have dollars . . . But in pesos *. . . And not much . . . But enough!"*

We chuckled for thinking the worst and profusely thanked the man for his generosity and apologizing that we had to turn down his invitation because the host family was expecting us back shortly.

This Isn't Complicated

Affordable long-term travel isn't complicated. We've covered four major tactics that you can use to save big money. If you travel and live by the following four rules, you'll be even better off:

1. Don't rush so much.

Traveling slower is more affordable and allows you to take more in. In most cases, you can travel at half the speed but twice as long for only a marginal increase in total cost. Long-term travel is a marathon and not a sprint. Focus more on being present and in the moment, and not always thinking about what's next.

2. Embrace conscious spending in all parts of your life, even while traveling.

We are all going to spend money, there's no real way around that—except for the extremist that forsakes all material possessions and the use of currency (they are out there). The key to living a rich life is to use your limited financial resources toward the things that matter most to you and cut spending on what isn't important.

3. Cook at least a little if you're looking to save money, but don't miss out on local cuisine.

If the food is nothing new, cook more often and save more money. When there is great local food to be had, indulge. It would be a shame to visit Thailand or Mexico and never eat the local food because you're holed up eating Top Ramen. But no matter where I'm traveling and how cheap it may be, I still always try to cook at least one meal per day (typically breakfast).

4. Work part time.

Part-time work can really stretch your timeline and potentially make your long-term travel sustainable indefinitely. There are many ways to go about this: seasonal work where you work half the year and travel the other (think: Alaska fisherman, Forest Service or National Park Service summer work), trade jobs which you can take anywhere (think: massage therapist, bartender, English teacher), web-based freelance work (writing and editing, web design, graphic design), or even the elusive passive income (rental property, stock dividends, YouTube videos, etc).

There are all manner of ways to reduce your expenses as you travel, and I have experimented with many others over the years. Still not convinced there are ways? Here are a few more quick and simple tactics:

Volunteering
WWOOFing
The World Wide Organization of Organic Farmers is a service that connects volunteers with local farmers. WWOOFing consists of volunteering with locals for a few hours of work each day in exchange for food and lodging, and can be a great addition to your travels if you are up for a little physical labor. The vast majority are rural farms, but not always, as there are eco-resorts and other types of institutions that use the service looking for volunteer help.

It can be a nice way to break up the travel experience if you've been stuck in cities or constantly on the go, it can help you learn the language working with locals, and you can learn many new things in the process.

I had never milked a goat in my life until WWOOFing on that small *finca* outside of San Gil, Colombia. During that particular WWOOFing assignment, we helped a family get a rural eco-hostel off the ground by building a solar shower, putting up signs, doing physical labor like building steps into a hillside, etc. We would be served breakfast, work for half a day, get lunch, work a little more, and then either relax or head to the neighborhood watering hole to chat with locals until dinner. It was a cheap and totally different way to experience rural Colombia for two weeks.

WWOOFing is available all over the world and is available to all ages. You just need to pay a small fee to receive the list and contact info of participating farms in each country and then reach out to them individually about possibilities. My experience was that they are generally quite receptive and don't require many specific skill sets beyond a willingness to help out and learn.

Work Away

There are alternatives to WWOOFing as well, for example Work Away. Work Away frequently receives high marks from both volunteers and the hosts. Work Away also doesn't cater solely to farming, but offers a wide range of volunteer opportunities.

We did a day of dog mushing in the frozen north of Fairbanks, Alaska, and our guide was an Australian volunteer who lived at the school and helped feed and care for the dozens of dogs at the kennel in exchange for room, board, and lessons to become a dog musher herself—all thanks to Work Away.

You can find opportunities manning the front desk at a local hostel, being a cook or deck hand aboard a sail boat in the Caribbean, working with organizations that rescue dogs on the streets of Cancun, and so much more.

Earthships

There are many volunteer movements in the burgeoning eco-friendly, sustainable, environmental realm—from housing to permaculture. Another project I took part in was building off the grid Earthships, which are self-sufficient eco-homes built with garbage that would otherwise end up in a landfill, like tires pounded with dirt for the walls, plastic bottles stuffed with garbage for insulation, and old glass bottles to provide colorful natural lighting in the ceiling.

This type of project was very physically demanding, but it was also particularly rewarding and educational since I had never before done anything like that. We worked alongside Aussies, Brits, gringos, Guatemalans, and Colombians, and the hard work and long days built strong bonds between all of the volunteers in a short amount of time.

Couchsurfing

There are also many other common tactics to enable long-term travel that I have yet to use or have much success with, yet they remain popular among other vagabonds like crashing on the couches of friendly strangers with Couchsurfing.

I have never had much success with Couchsurfing, but not for lack of trying. I've tried to use it on various occasions while traveling, but, for one reason or another, it just never works out. Maybe it's my beard. Plenty of other people love using the Couchsurfing platform, but I've always hit a dead end.

Beyond the actual couch sleeping aspect though, there is a highly active community behind Couchsurfing that regularly organizes social events throughout most cities around the world, and that is certainly something I would recommend checking out when you arrive in a new town.

The Biggest Reason You Won't Travel *Isn't* Money

All of these tactics (and more) are available to help you work around the ever-looming problem of money when you hope to travel more. Unfortunately none of these tactics can help you overcome the biggest obstacle you face in your goal to travel: yourself.

You probably don't need more ideas and more information—what you really need to do is just commit to making it happen. There is no perfect time to do it, and you could always have more money, better equipment, and there's always some excuse why you could wait.

Too many of us get overwhelmed thinking everything needs to be perfect first, and then "someday" we will make it happen, which leads us to doing absolutely nothing at all. Take it from those of us who've taken the leap: You don't have to have everything figured out; things will end up working out, and you won't regret it. You will, however, regret those things you didn't do or regret waiting so long.

Until one is committed, there is hesitancy, the chance to draw back, always ineffectiveness. Concerning all acts of initiative (and creation), there is one elementary truth the ignorance of which kills countless ideas and splendid plans: that the moment one definitely commits oneself, the providence moves too. A whole stream of events issues from the decision, raising in one's favor all manner of unforeseen incidents, meetings and material assistance, which no man could have dreamt would have come his way.

—W.H. Murray in *The Scottish Himalaya Expedition (1951)*

I recently finished an excellent book about writing a book (just like I hope to help you travel with this book, I needed help to actually finish writing it) called *Write. Publish. Repeat.* In it, the authors point out something that really resonated with me:

If it's not that easy, most people will decide it can't be done. If that last sentence seems absurd, think about people you know who want to lose weight or get in shape, including yourself. There isn't much more to it than 'burn more calories than you consume,' and that holds true for almost everyone. Weight loss takes effort and willpower, but it's not complicated. [. . .] They know what to do, but can't find ways to make themselves do the hard work required to make it happen. Almost everything you'd ever want to achieve is simple, but that doesn't mean it's easy.

—Sean Platt and Johnny B. Truant in *Write. Publish. Repeat.*

Breaking away from your current life to travel is really quite simple, but it certainly isn't easy. You've got the step-by-step directions to utilize all of the tactics mentioned in this book . . . The hard part is actually doing it and setting sail into the unknown, the new, and the uncomfortable.

The people who have known me the longest probably think it's easy for me to take off on another adventure, or tackle a crazy project like writing a novel, but the truth is that I'm terrified. I'm terrified of failure. I'm terrified of change. All I want to do is make a soft nest, eat doughnuts, and watch TV. It's fear of regrets, of squandering this one life, that motivates me. It's learning, over and over, that I'm always glad that I make this choice—that through the membrane of terror, there's a better place on the other side.

— Hugh Howey in *Wayfinder*

Resources and Further Reading

- Website: World Wide Opportunities on Organic Farms – wwoof.net

WWOOFing is a widespread and common resource for volunteers to connect with locals that need help. The work isn't particularly glamorous, but it is most likely interesting and fulfilling. You must purchases the lists of participating farms on a country-by-country basis.

- Website: Work Away – workaway.info

Work Away is an alternative to WWOOFing, which offers a greater variety of volunteer positions around the world. One plus is that membership is universal and not country specific as is WWOOFing.

- Website: CareTaker Gazette – caretaker.org

Caretaker Gazette is an online publication featuring a wide variety of care taking, house sitting, and volunteer positions around the world. The primary focus is working with properties like campgrounds, RV parks, resorts, etc. that are similar to, but more work intensive than, house sitting for private residences in that you will often be working with guests, doing routine maintenance and handyman work. Some feature a stipend or payment as well.

- Blog Post: Building Earthships Outside of Bogota

I volunteered with an organization called Long Way Home, a Guatemalan based organization, which builds eco-friendly Earthships at various projects around the world. Read more about my experience volunteering in Choachi, Colombia.

For links to all the resources and materials mentioned in this chapter, be sure to visit:

www.desktodirtbag.com/bigtravel-paperback

CHAPTER 8

FINDING SYNERGY

So there you have it! Four ways that I have personally used some unconventional travel hacks to stay on the road, stretch my budget, and travel for the long term.

I've lived out of the back of my pickup truck, traveling around the United States to some of the most iconic and beautiful natural areas on the planet to hike and climb. I've hacked the credit card game to save thousands on otherwise costly plane tickets. I rented a house in Medellin, Colombia, which I opened up to Airbnb guests to reduce my costs and live rent-free.

I've done WWOOFing for free food and housing. I've volunteered to build off the grid and eco-friendly Earthships out of tires and bottles.

I've cared for awesome pets from the suburbs of Seattle, to the remote mountains of Baja California, to the sprawling metropolis of Mexico City.

I'm always experimenting in ways to live a life full of experiences and on my own terms, in ways that don't require a trust fund to do it. I'd rather pursue a life rich in experiences instead of just pursuing riches.

Some approaches I've taken might not be desirable for the general populace (like living long term in the back of your truck), are harder to get started with (renting out a house on Airbnb in a foreign country), or require more physical labor (WWOOFing), whereas both the credit card travel hacking and house sitting gigs are easily doable by virtually anybody with an interest in travel, so long as they are responsible and want to get out more.

Now I hope you'll use at least one of these tactics to get out there on the road.

The Real Magic

But the real magic, I think, happens when you combine these methods within one big trip.

Want to take an overlanding road trip across the United States? You can break up the camping and road travel with house sitting opportunities as they present themselves on your journey. House sitting is also popular among the large expat community in Central America . . . Why not go for a longer drive?

Want to take a vacation from your big road trip with a two-week stint in Europe? Seek out a house sitting opportunity in London (one of the most frequently advertised house sitting locales with many opportunities), and use your frequent flier miles to redeem a round trip flight for less than 75,000 miles while only paying the government taxes.

And as Emeril would say—Bam! You've got yourself a two-week trip to London for the cost of your food and activities (and of course you can cook at your house sit). A trip like that would otherwise cost around $600 for a round trip flight, and at least $100 per night (probably much more) for a hotel ($1,400 in total for two weeks). But you just saved $2,000.

Use your free airline miles to book a one-way flight to a foreign country with no specific end date in mind. From there you can find a cheap place to rent for a few months, which you can rent out to other foreigners on Airbnb as you dive into the local culture, learn the language, and maybe start freelancing.

Freelancing, that's the other big "secret" to be able to stay on the road forever and break out of that "work, save money, travel, run out of money, then repeat" model. But alas, that is a subject I've saved for another book—visit www.desktodirtbag.com/freelancebook for more info about how even just a little side hustle can transform your travel plans massively.

The travel hacks that we've gone into in this book are not just meant to be used individually, choosing either one or the other. No, the real magic happens, in my eyes, when you combine them and employ all the tricks in the bag. Each tactic outlined here when used by itself will provide you with a Big Win and save you hundreds, but the synergistic effect when combined is where you can save not just hundreds, but many thousands of dollars.

And that is exactly what has kept me on the road for so long.

Prioritize Today

I prioritized travel and adventure above other more conventional things like a mortgage, stability, and routine. There's nothing wrong with those things, if that's what you really want (and not just what you're "supposed to do"). But something tells me you long to get out there and travel, maybe for a few months or maybe for longer.

That's why you're reading this book after all, isn't it?

You've got real-world actionable tactics, but now it's time to turn them into a reality.

You've almost made it through this book. You've got the information you need to save some serious money when you travel. Now it's time to take at least one real, actionable step *today* to get your future travel plans off the ground.

Here's what you can do today:

- *Credit Card Mileage Game*

This is pretty much the easiest way to get started and provides a definite Big Win, even if you don't yet have immediate plans to use the miles. Visit www.CardsforTravel.com, find the current best offers available, and apply for the card.

- *Overlanding*

Scour the Internet and search for information about "overlanding" along with whatever make or model of car you have. Somebody has probably already done it and shared their experiences and setup. If your vehicle truly isn't well suited to the overlanding life, then take a look at the Top 10 Most Popular Overlanding Vehicles, and see how much you could sell your vehicle for on KelleyBlueBook.com.

- *Airbnb*

Sign up for an Airbnb account, and request your first character references from friends and family. If you're new to Airbnb, you'll get $25 toward your first stay as a guest just for signing up with my link (www.desktodirtbag.com/airbnb), so you're already saving a little on a future stay. If you have space in your current place, list it. If you don't have extra space you can always list a "make me move" price to rent your whole apartment and then crash at a friend's house when someone books.

- *House Sitting*

Create an account and profile on TrustedHouseSitters.com or HouseCarers.com, and start building up your references from friends and family while seeking out your first real house sitting opportunity locally. Having solid references now will help you land that dream gig in the future. You can save 20% off of your Trusted House Sitters membership by using my link to sign up (www.desktodirtbag.com/housesitters).

Step-by-Step

All of the above steps are easy to take and ones you can do today with no excuses. Remember: Taking imperfect action today beats the perfect plan "someday."

Every little step of progress you make will get you one step closer to your big travel plans and make those vague plans start to feel more concrete.

The Ideal Trip

My next piece of advice to you would be to start planning your ideal trip. Really flesh it out.

Don't just say, "I hope to travel someday," but rather, "I aim to backpack across Central America for six months, exactly one year from now."

The more concrete your goal, the better guidance you have to make it happen. Maybe you change directions once you are out there, but at least you're on the way. Think of it like a GPS—if you don't tell it where you want to go, it can't tell you how to get there. Now go write it down by hand and put it where you'll see it. Seriously.

I really hope that some of what I've included here has already proved helpful to you and opened your eyes to the possibility of affordable long-term travel. There will always be more naysayers than action takers, but if I can help even a fraction of you reading this book to actually get out there on the road, then I can consider this a success.

Will you be one of those people?

If you have any questions, suggestions, or just want to say hello, please drop me an email at ryan@desktodirtbag.com—I read every email and try to respond to everyone, though it can take a while depending on my travel schedule and Internet connectivity.

If you've found this book helpful, please be sure to leave a quick and honest review on Amazon.com—just visit www.desktodirtbag.com/travelbook-review to be redirected to the review page. Reviews are the lifeblood of the author on Amazon, and every single one helps; it need not be a lengthy treatise either.

If you haven't already, don't forget to visit www.desktodirtbag.com/bigtravel-paperback for links to all the resources mentioned throughout this book and some bonus materials which will further help you turn your travel dreams into a reality.

Happy travels,

Ryan
www.desktodirtbag.com

ABOUT THE AUTHOR

Ryan is an author, blogger, and traveler that will always call the Pacific Northwest home even though he hasn't really lived there since 2007. His online home can be found at www.desktodirtbag.com, where he blogs about finding adventure and the pursuit of location independence. It is also where he implores his readers to GO OUTSIDE— because life is too short to watch it pass by from a desk . . .

Like many others, he got his first real taste of long-term travel during college as he studied abroad in both Italy and Yemen.

He left college with big dreams of adventure before he ended up moving across the country to Washington, DC, where he worked as a legislative assistant for a senior member of Congress and passed the vast majority of each day sedentary. After his job came to an end, he launched himself into the world of vagabonding and hasn't looked back.

You can connect with Ryan on Instagram

@desktodirtbag, where he shares photos of his travels or on Twitter @desktodirtbag. Feel free to send him an email at ryan@desktodirtbag.com because he loves hearing from his readers. And he swears he normally never writes in the third person . . .

Other Books by Ryan

To see all of Ryan's currently available books (and be notified of those in the works), please visit www.desktodirtbag.com/mybooks

One last thing …

Like you, this book wants to travel. After you've read this book be sure to pass it off to a friend, take it with you traveling and leave it in a "take one, leave one" library in your hostel dorm or overseas campground. Don't let it languish on your bookshelf and be yet another physical object holding you back from travel.

Made in the USA
Middletown, DE
09 April 2022